The Multiple Identities of the Reception Teacher

SAGE was founded in 1965 by Sara Miller McCune to support the dissemination of usable knowledge by publishing innovative and high-quality research and teaching content. Today, we publish over 900 journals, including those of more than 400 learned societies, more than 800 new books per year, and a growing range of library products including archives, data, case studies, reports, and video. SAGE remains majority-owned by our founder, and after Sara's lifetime will become owned by a charitable trust that secures our continued independence.

Los Angeles | London | New Delhi | Singapore | Washington DC | Melbourne

The Multiple Identities of the Reception Teacher

Pedagogy and Purpose

Edited by **Anna Cox** and **Gillian Sykes**

SAGE | LearningMatters

Los Angeles | London | New Delhi
Singapore | Washington DC | Melbourne

Learning Matters
An imprint of SAGE Publications Ltd
1 Oliver's Yard
55 City Road
London EC1Y 1SP

SAGE Publications Inc.
2455 Teller Road
Thousand Oaks, California 91320

SAGE Publications India Pvt Ltd
B 1/I 1 Mohan Cooperative Industrial Area
Mathura Road
New Delhi 110 044

SAGE Publications Asia-Pacific Pte Ltd
3 Church Street
#10-04 Samsung Hub
Singapore 049483

Editor: Amy Thornton
Production controller: Chris Marke
Project management: Deer Park Productions
Marketing manager: Lorna Patkai
Cover design: Wendy Scott
Typeset by: C&M Digitals (P) Ltd, Chennai, India
Printed and bound by CPI Group (UK) Ltd,
Croydon, CR0 4YY

Library of Congress Control Number: 2016933147

British Library Cataloguing in Publication Data

A catalogue record for this book is available from the
British Library.

ISBN 978-1-4739-5952-1 (pbk)
ISBN 978-1-4739-5951-4

Contents

Introduction to the editors and authors

Introduction to the editors

Anna Cox is the programme leader for a PGCE programme at the University of Northampton, training teachers to work with children from 3 to 7 years of age. She teaches on BA and PGCE programmes for primary and early years trainees. She previously worked at Sheffield Hallam University, for Derbyshire County Council Early Years Support Team and Tameside Borough Childcare and Education Team over the past 20 years. She has particular interests in supporting those who teach the youngest children and in teachers' self-efficacy.

Gillian Sykes is Senior lecturer in Education, Early Years at the University of Northampton teaching on the BA Early Years, PGCE 3–7 and PGCE 0–5 programmes. Professional interests in early years education include: enabling environments, learning outdoors, the arts and creativity and supporting young children's writing development. Specialised in the field of early years as a teacher, lead teacher, forest school practitioner, mentor and Local Authority Early Years senior advisor. Now supporting the development of early years teachers in 'community of practice'-based CPD projects.

Introduction to the authors

Eleonora Teszenyi is a Senior Lecturer in early years education at the University of Northampton. Before entering Higher Education she had worked in the early years sector for 19 years as a nursery practitioner, Early Years teacher/Early Years professional, Early Years advisor and children centre teacher. Her specialist area is child development (birth to 5 years) and her current research projects include work on mixed and same-age groups in Hungarian kindergartens. Her other interests are related to parent partnerships and work-based learners in higher education.

Julia Beckreck has a wealth of experience in the field of education. Having originally trained at Goldsmith College, and then teaching in both England and the United States, she has endeavoured to understand how children learn and how to provide them with the fullest support and care to reach their own goals. More recently, her headship in Leicestershire and, after retirement, as a children's centre teacher, both afforded her opportunities to observe children and adults learning and teaching together.

Shona Lewis is a visiting tutor at Birmingham City University supporting early years students on the Teacher First programme. She is also a county moderator for Warwickshire and an associate lecturer at University of Northampton. Professional interests in early years education include literacy and assessment. She worked as a classroom teacher, early years co-ordinator, literacy co-ordinator, senior leader, associate literacy teacher, county moderator, for the local authority as a senior early years advisory teacher leading on assessment and literacy, and was programme manager of Teach First Primary at The University of Leicester.

Claire Underwood is the Nursery teacher, EYFS leader and Assistant Headteacher at Eastfield Academy in Northampton. She is in her tenth year of teaching and is passionate about child-centred learning. She embraces outdoor learning and demonstrates a great commitment to developing Forest School and outdoor activities throughout the school. Keen to share her enthusiasm for early years she can be found collaborating with colleagues as far away as Bologna and Barnsley but can be mostly found on Twitter and her nursery blog.

Samantha Weeks is currently the director of Early Years at Stamford Junior School and a Reception class teacher. She is acting as a 'champion of research' at school and maintains her relationship with the University of Northampton where she was previously a senior lecturer in education, Early Years. Before lecturing Samantha enjoyed a range of Early Years positions including Reception and nursery teaching, Children's Centre teacher and a Local Authority Advisory teacher: always with an emphasis on the Arts. After studying for an MA at the Institute of Education she was lucky enough to visit Reggio Emilia and has never been the same again! Her specialist areas include expressive arts as a form of communication, the way in which children engage with clay and embracing a rights-based approach to teaching.

Introduction

This book has been created by a community of writers, all passionate about young children's learning. Our experiences include Reception practice in the 1980s, 1990s, 2000s and into the twenty-first century and our total of years of Reception practice is better not revealed! Our decision to write this book was based on the fact that we believe the Reception Year is a fascinating and exciting year for children and their teachers. This does not diminish what has come before, or indeed what comes after, but celebrates the 'magic bit in the middle'. Our discussions are often based around the complex nature of the role of the Reception teacher and the variety of 'hats' worn each day or each week through the year. Reception teachers metamorphose into and out of roles and identities as different situations arise. It is these many roles that this book seeks to unravel.

As authors we make no excuse for this book being written 'from the heart'. We recognise that the best Reception teachers are those who are 'emotionally connected' to the work they do, always striving for excellence. They are the teachers who cannot, and would not choose to, separate care from education. At all times they place the child and their well-being at the centre of all they do. We have often heard it said that the Reception year is a bridge into Key Stage 1; this can mean that it is devalued and seen only as a time of transition and preparation for something greater and more important. If the bridge analogy is in any way relevant to this book we must think of bridges in different ways. Firstly, bridges are vital in making way from one place to another and so it may be in the Reception Year. However, there have been times in history when bridges also provided other more varied experiences – with shops, chapels, markets and other activities bringing them to life. Bridges are varied and intriguing in design, bearing their travellers with care, but offering opportunities for risk taking, and diversity in mode and movement dependent upon the traveller. Such is the image of a Reception class and its teacher: each different, each unique and each responding to the needs of the children and their families.

We want to celebrate the way that teachers bring to life the Reception Year and we have conceptualised the Reception Year differently. An alternative image is to see the Reception Year as an opportunity for *time travel* and a time for children to have experiences which acknowledge their younger selves and which support their development as individuals.

Reception teachers facilitate the time travel of their classes and help them to make progress towards the people they will become, building on past experiences and creating new ones. They help children learn to be robust, to face challenges and to be able to cope with new experiences in the school context and beyond. For that reason, this book is not curriculum focused (though the key themes which are considered can all be enacted successfully following the Early Years Foundation Stage guidance). There are many books which unpick the content of the curriculum; in this book it is our aim to unpick and explore the role of the Reception teacher, and their many identities without using the curriculum as a framework.

Why is this? We consider that Reception teachers fulfil a role which has a strong public face and one in which the boundaries of professional and personal identity can be blurred. How many Reception teachers have been invited to tea at a child's home or to a birthday party? This brings into conflict personal and professional values – should such invitations be accepted or turned down? Every Reception teacher knows that they are observed and judged, however informally. Cultural context plays a part too, with some environments where teachers are respected and even venerated. They are the source of example and inspiration for children and families. Many young learners on the African continent and in China are brought up with an elevated view of teachers. There are those who suggest that this is not the case in the United Kingdom, and indeed it is not so clearly demonstrated through the media and the pronouncements of politicians. However, many adults remember their own Reception teachers fondly and hope for the most positive and supportive Reception teachers for their own children. So, in this book we look at the ways in which the perception and the reality of a Reception teacher's role are formed, and how a Reception teacher's self-worth can be acknowledged and supported.

Many Reception teachers reflect on what their role is in the school context, sometimes undervalued by colleagues who teach older children and viewed as less encumbered by planning and assessment. Through the pages of this book we want to encourage Reception teachers to reflect also on their important roles in the lives of children and families, and the wider community. Sometimes this is understood by locating Reception teachers in their spheres of influence and action, such as the ecological systems theory put forward by Bronfenbrenner (1979, p.21). In this book an alternative model is provided for understanding *who* Reception teachers are in the lives of children, families and school communities. In a straw poll of Reception teachers the words used to describe themselves and the features of their role included carer, educator, key person, friend, play partner, more knowledgeable other. This list too is expanded upon later in the book, where is it linked to the children's skills, knowledge and attributes in the Reception year, always working in line and in tune with what is happening in the child's life. The best Reception teachers look for and find children's strengths, interests, capabilities and more and they build on them.

So, in this Introduction we set out the vision of the book and its structure along with suggestions for different ways in which to access it. These suggestions for the way that the book can be used, to make it useful and enjoyable to the reader include the use of the blank page at the end of each chapter for personal notes. The book is designed to be used as a working document: written in, jotted on, highlighted and thumbed by those who use it. Some

Figure Intro.1 Close co-operation between a Reception teacher and young learners

may choose to read through from the front to the back, and then revisit key issues. It is more likely that dipping in to chapters or sections which relate to current practice issues will be effective for individual readers straight away. Vignettes, talks and tasks for the team, nuggets of further inspiration and points to ponder are also included at various points in the text, and these can function as a stimulus on their own or following on from reading the chapters that contain them. The book takes an innovative view of teaching in the Reception year and so the content is presented in a particular way, alongside some theoretical underpinnings relevant to the individual chapters. The chapters reflect the characters of the writers and so they are not uniform in structure and approach but each one has been written with passion by the writer or writers responsible for it. Opinions and viewpoints will vary and will be a source of respectful debate. However, these are opinions and viewpoints which are based on years of critical reflection.

This book is intended for anyone interested in the role of the Reception teacher. It is hoped that it may be used to develop discussion among and between those working or training in the Reception year. We think this is a book where the more experienced Reception teacher will be able to find comfort and challenge. We also urge that the book is used to spark discussion with colleagues teaching in Key Stages 1 and 2 and beyond. Perhaps those who think we are 'just playing'? Thinking back to the analogy of a bridge, then, we imagine Reception teachers on a magnificent rope bridge with colleagues and giving it a good 'wobble'! We want to shake and reshape people's perceptions of the Reception teacher, and for them to appreciate its diverse and multifaceted nature. Who else would go home at the end of the day having had half a cup of cold coffee, a bit of carrot (from the snack bar), wearing a row of wooden threading beads, covered in paint, clutching a note from an earnest four year old reminding you to bring in 'flawr, solt, and oyl'? Such is the life of the Reception teacher.

The structure of the book is as follows:

Chapter 1 – Anna Cox and Eleonora Teszenyi

Time travel, kaleidoscopes and a hat shop. Here the notion of multiple identities of the Early Years teacher is unpicked. In this chapter a range of possible models for the Reception teacher are explored. A further model created by the authors is proposed and explored. In this chapter the reader will be able to access ideas about Reception practice to add to their existing ideas and experience or to challenge them and also be able to engage with a more dynamic and flexible conception of the role.

Chapter 2 – Eleonora Teszenyi

Children at four. What is it to be a four year old? This is an in-depth chapter, deliberately longer and more theoretically based than the others. This was an informed decision as without understanding what it is like to be a four or five year old, we cannot begin to identify, justify and shape our roles.

Chapter 3 – Samantha Weeks

You as an advocate for Early Childhood. Fiercely protective of the importance which needs to be placed on Early Years education, this chapter explores the role of the twenty-first century Reception teacher in 'fighting the corner' for teaching and learning in this critical period of a child's life.

Chapter 4 – Claire Underwood, Anna Cox and Gillian Sykes

You as a collaborator in learning. This chapter is steeped in personal practice. Here you will find fine examples of adventuring in learning with young children, and the synergy that is created as you become partners in generating new knowledge and understanding.

Chapter 5 – Samantha Weeks and Claire Underwood

You as a creator of the learning environment. This chapter explores the relationship between pedagogy and knowledge of child development in the organisation of the learning environment. It validates the need to involve the children in this creation and draws on the work of Malaguzzi, Rinaldi and Jarman to help us develop our own child-centred environments.

Chapter 6 – Gillian Sykes

You as a landscape architect. This chapter prioritises the unique qualities of the outdoors as a learning environment vital to young children's development. It reflects on past and current theory to help us justify and plan for our own outdoors. Again, we highlight the need to listen to the voice of the child as we become architects of these diverse, ever changing environments.

Chapter 7 – Shona Lewis and Julia Beckreck

You as an auditor of children's learning. This chapter begins 'We see children's development by what they do. They construct their own learning. Yet how do we observe, understand and respond?' It leads us on a path, filled with corners and bends, where we tune into the children we work with. It elevates this often-maligned aspect of our practice as we rejoice in what we see, and then do.

Chapter 8 – Gillian Sykes

You as a partner in the lives of children, families and communities. In this chapter we look at the many people who affect and effect the lives of the children with whom we work. This chapter seeks to promote these partnerships and takes a positive stance in making these relationships work for the benefit of the children in our care.

Chapter 9 – Anna Cox

You in a team of researchers. In this chapter some different ways of looking at learning through reflection and research are talked about. You are encouraged to see the children as researchers in a community of practice. The importance of researching your own practice and of CPD are also discussed.

Chapter 10 – Anna Cox and Gillian Sykes

The mirror in the hat shop. These are the closing remarks for now. We briefly revisit some of the ideas from the chapters and hope to send you off into an optimistic future.

As you delve into the book you will find it has a range of features which vary from chapter to chapter. There are some vignettes through which contemporary practice is exemplified and examined. We also include a 'points to ponder' to encourage personal reflection and review of experience in the light of ideas in the text. These are the most personal of the inclusions, not designed to change practice but to have confidence that personal professional practice is supported by sound judgement. We have also included some 'Further inspiration' where particular ideas are shared, web links noted, supplies or resources highlighted and other good things. Many may be known to readers already but others may not and so it seemed a good idea to share the things that excite us. Therefore, features of the text are:

Brief bullet points which offer an overview of what the chapter will cover

Point to ponder – ideas to challenge your own thinking

Team talks and tasks – these will help you to work as a team to become a true community of practice

Vignettes – examples of contemporary practice to bring aspects of the chapter to life

Further inspiration – ideas which have inspired us and we hope, in turn, will inspire you

References – to further support your personal knowledge and understanding

Jottings – a space to note points for interest or action.

To bring to a close this Introduction it is important to be explicit: the philosophy that underpins this book is based on a competence model of the child, based on understanding children's developing bodies and minds during this important year. This concurs with what Dubiel (2014, p.66) describes as 'socially just and child centred practice'. We can explain our approach by adopting his term 'a value prism' – we believe that children are curious and idiosyncratic, capable and enquiring, and full of possibility. This is the reason that the role of the Reception teacher is challenging and fulfilling as well as very important. The writing team who have produced this book share the view that Reception teachers are important and special people in the lives of children.

References

Bronfenbrenner, U. (1979) *The ecology of human development.* Cambridge, MA: Harvard University Press.

Dubiel, J. (2014) *Effective assessment in the Early Years Foundation Stage.* Early Excellence: London.

1 Time travel, kaleidoscopes and a hat shop

Anna Cox and Eleonora Teszenyi

In this chapter we will begin to consider:

- models and ideas about the identities and roles of a Reception teacher, including Bronfenbrenner's ecological systems theory and 'the hierarchy of the heart and the head';
- new ways of looking at the roles to support a personally negotiated understanding;
- child-centred pedagogical approaches and care-full practice;
- the social construction of the teaching role;
- the different hats teachers wear according to the roles they fulfil in children's lives.

Starting points

The demands and pressures on the teaching profession are influenced by political change, and this cannot be avoided. The most successful Reception teachers fend off the favours and fancies that come about from this. Good teaching can become a contested notion in a climate of change and teachers need to be able to defend their own good practice. This will come from a strong sense of 'who you are as a teacher' and more specifically for the purposes of this book 'who you are as a Reception teacher'. In this book the term multiple identities is used as a concept that portrays a range of personal and professional roles within an educational context. This poses the questions 'what is identity?' and 'what is role?'. By identity we mean a sense of self, developed from experiences across a range of contexts – personal, professional and cultural, for example – which is ever evolving and changing through the life course. The notion of role is less dynamic and is the label given to a set of functions, and so is the practical and utilitarian aspect of identity. So, a Reception teacher can be seen to have a complex and interlinked set of identities and roles. In this chapter these ideas are explored and new ideas generated. It is important to remember that multiple identities are not fixed nor are they shared among Reception teachers. They evolve, are negotiated and change; they are deeply personal. Some of the features discussed in this chapter will resonate with you and others less so. Over time some of the features you relate to will take centre stage and then they will recede – who you are as a Reception teacher is always in flux. The value of discussing the many identities is to help individual teachers to identify and develop their own identity as a teacher of the Reception year. It should also help to reassure you that it is wholly appropriate that your work is an integral part of who you are as a person and as a professional.

Team talks and tasks

Ask everyone in your team to write down five words that capture parts of their roles in the Reception classroom. Share the lists and combine them to make a master list. Use this to help you to clarify your shared purposes in the classroom.

One of a number of existing models is proposed by Rose and Rogers (2012) who unpick the role of Early Years practitioners into components. They suggest Early Years practitioners act as: critical reflector, carer, communicator, facilitator, observer, assessor and creator. This 'plural practitioner' (p.5) has undoubtedly shaped our thinking. The roles that they propose are recognisable in Reception teachers but do not cover all that it means to be an effective Reception teacher. We have expanded some of the categories here and others are left for your consideration (facilitator, observer, assessor and creator). Their first component, the skill of reflection, will undoubtedly have been highlighted throughout your training. Once in practice you are more likely to wake up thinking about how to redesign your role-play area than to use a reflective model to do this – it will be in your blood! The second Rose and Rogers category, the Reception teacher as a carer, is explored more fully in a later section of this chapter, but at this point it is sufficient to say that caring *about* the children in your class will go alongside caring *for* them but must always be done in the context of a vision of the strong child, not one based on viewing the child as a collection of needs to be met. The next role in the list, the teacher as a communicator, is explored very fully in other chapters and so does not warrant much additional comment. The importance and diversity of communication does allow us to explore briefly just how skilful young children are at reading our faces. An often-mentioned expression is that 'eyes are the windows of the soul' – this is thought to be part of a quotation from Hiram Powers (an American sculptor, 1805–1873). He said 'The eye is the window of the soul, the mouth the door. The intellect, the will, are seen in the eye; the emotions, sensibilities, and affections, in the mouth'. The children in your class will be very able to attend to your features and learn a lot about you and for some of them what they read there will set the tone for their day.

The Rose and Rogers model of Early Years practitioners can shed some light on what it is to be a Reception teacher but you are a distinct group among Early Years practitioners. Below, in the point to ponder, another model is reviewed and commented on, as a further step on the journey to unpick the multiple identities of the Reception teacher.

Point to ponder

Hiram Powers

Try to find an image of the sculpture 'fisher boy' by Hiram Powers. The figure is a nude holding a shell to his ear. Take a close look at the shell and at the child's face. Can you think of an activity for your children stimulated by this image or another of Hiram's works?

Hierarchy of needs to hierarchy of the heart and the head

The well-known hierarchy of needs (Maslow, 1954) has been revisited by Robinson (2007, p.10) to support practitioners who work with the youngest children. Here we use the term 'hierarchy of the heart and the head' to describe this model and reflect on it from the perspective of Reception teachers. As can be seen from Figure 1.1 overleaf it rests on the personal passion of the Reception teacher; a person who has chosen and wants to work with the youngest children in the school context. Working with young children whom you care for should allow you to be your authentic self, to share with them the person that you really are. All Reception teachers are different and they manifest their personalities as teachers and as people in different ways. What is really important is that you should be the Reception teacher that you know you can and should be. This is one of the things that make the role both draining and sustaining, challenging and affirming. You may be the butt of jokes about playing all day in the sand or not being able to count to more than ten; prejudice about working with the youngest children still exists in schools. This is discussed more fully later.

This hierarchy of the heart and the head reveals a person who in their practice creates sensitive relationships and high quality interactions; understanding the link between education and care for children who may be away from their familiar adults for longer in a school day than they have ever been before. An ethos of edu-care and a child-centred playful pedagogy

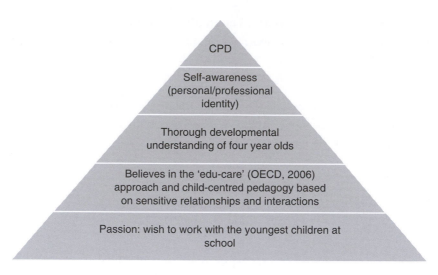

Figure 1.1 The basis for the 'hierarchy of the heart and the head'

must be embraced by Reception teachers; both suit a Reception teacher both personally and professionally. This is where the personal and professional identity merges the most. Think, for example, about the sense of security demonstrated by young children to a degree where they call teachers 'mummy' and invite them to their house for a play or birthday party. This depth of relationship with a young child is a real privilege but not one that is widely understood by others. Care roles are not valued as highly as the roles associated with education even though the expectations are that children develop lifelong learning skills in their earlier years of schooling to ensure they become useful citizens of our society. Creating the balance between care and education within their pedagogical approach to children places demands on Reception teachers more so than those of any other year group.

Alongside all this, the heart and the head of our Reception teacher need to be full of secure knowledge of child development and in particular a deep and always evolving understanding of four year olds. The significance of the developmental understanding of four year olds is fully explained and explicitly stated in Chapter 2. The Reception teacher's application of pedagogy must be in line with a full understanding of the children in the Reception classroom. One of the phrases which draws out the importance of the work of the Reception teacher is that we should always consider children as 'beings' and not mere 'becomings', somehow less important and worthy of all that is best in the world than adults are. Focus always on a credit model of the child that relies on the understanding of children's strengths and interests and avoid the energy-sapping deficit model where the focus of attention is on what the children cannot do or have not developed yet.

As the model indicates, self-awareness too is crucial. It is essential partly because it is a precursor for self-assuredness and resilience in the politically changing world of education.

In addition, it is essential because self-awareness gives reassurance to Reception teachers to rely on their instincts to do the best for and by the child. This is particularly needed because developmentally children in a Reception class are on such a broad spectrum. A resilient teacher, who is self-aware and self-assured, can interpret curriculum expectations and local or national drives/initiatives in light of what is best for the children who are actually in the class at any given time. They practise intuitively from a self-assured stance so they can justify decisions. You need to understand yourself from both a personal and professional perspective – as these aspects of identity play out strongly in the intimate relationships of the Reception classroom.

Nurturing the Reception teacher's soul is something we believe in strongly and it is part of the purpose of this book, so continuous professional development tops the hierarchy for the heart and the head. A model for the Reception teacher reflects the importance of this year in children's lives and the positive choices made to do this job. For the authors of this book the Reception year is full of vital opportunities, not something that happens between nursery or pre-school and the start of the National Curriculum. You will thrive most when you are driven by professional and personal reflections and by the desire to self-actualise; to reach full potential as a Reception teacher, not just as a teacher of any ages.

Team talks and tasks

When you have had a tough day and need a 'little lift' think about the passion for working with young children that brought you in to Reception teaching. How would you share this in a tweet of 140 characters?

Revisiting Bronfenbrenner and giving him a shake

A well-established approach to understanding roles is the ecological systems theory by Bronfenbrenner (1979). Here we locate his ideas in a complex and multi-layered ecological system. This can be conceptualised as the external factors which shape or at least influence the identity of the Reception teacher from outside. So, the hierarchy of the heart and the head model above relates to the intrinsic factors which shape us. Bronfenbrenner is well known for his proposal of five ecological systems and here this is revisited with the Reception teacher at the centre. The micro-system in psychological proximity to the individual appears at the core – for the Reception teacher that might be the immediate environment of the class. That is the domain in which a Reception teacher's most important professional relationships lie. In the classroom you can be empowered and nurtured by the children and have the opportunity to grow into the Reception teacher you are supposed to be. You are a unique teacher with your group of four and five year olds around you. The exciting thing about the micro-system is that how you treat those children will greatly impact how they respond to you. Each child's special temperament will be important to you.

The meso-system around it describes how the parts of the micro-system work together with you at its heart. The emotional climate of the classroom, the respect you show to the children and your commitment to inclusion are key to the meso-system that is usually called your school. Here your own interpretation of the role will come into play; some Reception teachers are bubbly and loud, others are calm and tranquil and the best can be all of these things and can find their way between them to benefit the children.

The exo-system is the level at which other people and places impact a Reception teacher who does not interact with them directly. For example, in a school in an alliance of local schools there may be influences which filter down to particular teachers explicitly or otherwise. The impact of local authority initiatives and school networks or clusters fit into this layer of influences.

? Point to ponder

What is the exo-system that influences how you function as a Reception teacher in your current context? Is your school part of an academy chain? Are you part of a cluster group? Is yours a faith school? How do such features influence your practice and are you able to honour your beliefs and principles?

The macro-system is often described as the largest and most remote set of people and things that relate to the individual but which still have a strong influence. For most Reception teachers this is most likely to be the national educational system in which your school operates. Interestingly, this is the level at which relative freedoms for the Reception teacher can be explored; for example, the relative freedom or otherwise allowed by the legally defined curriculum and the impact of the community in which the school is located. These things can affect you either positively or negatively and must be negotiated to allow you to function effectively and undertake 'care-full practice' (Luff and Kanyal, 2015). These authors describe a model of practice in Early Years settings derived from and supported by many of the giants in early childhood upon whose shoulders we stand today. They reflect on the view of Pestalozzi, who in his approach to educational practice saw the possibility to improve the human race, and on Montessori's deeply held view that conflict resolution, unity among peoples and the establishment of lasting world peace was the work of education (1946, 1949, 1992). These ambitions remind the Reception teacher to keep eyes up, so that the horizon full of potential is in sight.

Point to ponder

Finding your own 'care-full practice'

By 'care-full' practice we mean practice that is respectful of children and sees them as active and engaged members of a learning community. We mean practice that acknowledges but is not limited by differences in individual development. We mean practice which is whole hearted and generous but not sentimental. Practice from the head, the heart and the hands. It is important that you have and continually revisit your own vision of 'care-full practice'. Create an image or write a poem to capture some key elements of your 'care-full practice'. There is a space at the end of the chapter where you can do this.

Returning to Bronfenbrenner, there is one more system to consider. The chrono-system adds the useful dimension of time, which allows the influence of both change and constancy in your environment to be revisited. Chrono-system changes can have an enormous impact on the role of a Reception teacher – the movement of migrants across Europe from other parts of the world provides a contemporary example. Also part of the chrono-system are political changes such as government changes at a general election. In this book the political context is not a key consideration; this is not because it is not important but because we believe it is possible to be the best teacher you can be in any political climate. All Early Years practitioners, including Reception teachers, have experience and skills to 'fly under the radar' to achieve the best for children.

Bronfenbrenner also highlights the role of networks and how agency for the individual comes from being located within cultural, social, political and historical contexts. Many Reception teachers will be able to locate themselves in these nested systems. Also from Bronfenbrenner's work is his notion of 'ecological transitions' (p.6) – changes in role or setting, which occur throughout the life course. Reception teachers, as time travellers, undertake ecological transitions at an altogether higher speed. Such transitions are frequent in the term, the week and often the day of a Reception teacher. They are also frequent in the lives of children in the class with the arrival of a new sibling, moving house or joining the 'after school club'. The children's ecological transitions impact on the teacher too. Sometimes both teacher and child are involved in transition at the same time but for different reasons. You will face transition to being the teacher of a completely different class of children each year, for example.

One of the ways to view the interplay of ecological transitions and the role of the Reception teacher is to imagine it as a kaleidoscope. The view is ever changing and the balance between the elements is in flux as the ring is turned – this is perhaps more like the changing roles, responsibilities and responses of the Reception teacher. Bronfenbrenner's model is useful in showing some of the multi-coloured shards in the Reception teacher kaleidoscope, stimulating thought about influences on the Reception teacher and the spheres in which they move. However, it feels too static, or at least too ordered, to be really representative of the multiple identities of the Reception teacher.

Caring by choice

Hargreaves placed emotions at the centre of teachers' work (1994, 1998) and this is no less the case today. There is no reason to think that this will change any time soon. Reception teachers enter a private world with their classes and they invest themselves in it. The investment is emotional, psychological and cultural. Sometimes it can also be financial! Most Reception teachers we know want to share good things with the children they teach and cannot resist new and exciting resources for example. Their homes are full of items linked to their professional practice and this indicates the strong link between the professional identity of teachers and their personal identity, the very people that they are.

Teaching involves strong feelings of protecting and supporting, and immense emotional labour – labour of love. Because of the developmental stage Reception-age children are at, this dimension of teaching is fundamental in children's healthy development and progress. Positive responsiveness, mindfulness and empathic engagement are key components of a Reception teacher's professional identity; these are some of the things that make a Reception teacher distinctly different from teachers of other ages. These essential characteristics are directly aligned with the developmental needs of four year olds. Reception teachers are drawn to young children through emotion (Moyles, 2010). Predictability of care from the teacher and the classroom assistant, sensitivity, patience and kindness are ingredients of the love you offer children. This is something that not all teachers are comfortable to acknowledge.

Professional love is not a notion much explored in the UK context, though it is more widely understood in some European countries. Some languages, such as Hungarian, distinguish between love for children in a professional context (*szeretet*) and love between people in relationships (*szerelem*). Two different terms are used for a kiss Early Years practitioners might give to children in their care (*puszi*) and for a kiss in a more sexual context (*csók*). Love in the Early Years context has been considered by Page (2011) and is the focus of the PLEYS study (Professional Love in Early Years Settings study). The study is located in work with the youngest children and those in private, voluntary and independent childcare settings. It is our view that the issue remains crucial further into children's experiences with adults outside their families and is certainly important for Reception teachers. Our contact with children can, and to the authors of this book should, be both physically and emotionally intimate. Loving children in a way that does not threaten or undermine parental love and in a way that is appropriate in a professional context is demanding. It is a dynamic act as opposed to it being passive and not everyone can do it. Robinson (2007) points out, it is not what you do but HOW you do it. The child is mapped out in your mind so that the warmth and care you offer is tailored to the child's needs and reflects acceptance and respect. This is more a human response than a pedagogic one, and highly appropriate to the Reception teacher role. In this way Reception teachers are able to hold children's emotions for them and help them to develop strategies for emotional self-regulation (as discussed in the emotional development section of Chapter 2).

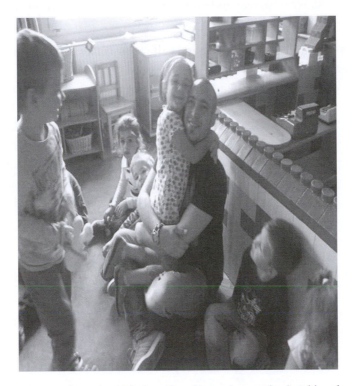

Figure 1.2 Reception teachers should feel comfortable to show professional love for children they teach

Multiple identities and your view of yourself

Thinking about the multiple identities of a Reception teacher can be liberating and should allow you to construct an individualised professional identity, reflecting your professional values and beliefs, often very closely aligned to personal values. Griffin, researching identity among health professionals, considers professional identities to be 'the intersection where the outside world meets the individual' (2008, p.356). Taking this idea into education does reveal some of the ways in which Reception teacher identity is formed. Families of the children you teach will hold views about what a Reception teacher can and should be. These are often a reflection of personal experience, whether this was good or bad. In addition, colleagues, governors, inspection agencies and members of other related professions all hold views about what a Reception teacher is. A similar notion was noted by Goldstein at the end of the twentieth century. She berated the 'erroneous conception of early childhood educators as somehow not as professional or not as intelligent as teachers of older children' (Goldstein, 1998, p.245). It was her view that the humanistic approaches that underpin 'care-full education' are certainly not less valuable than other curriculum-directed phases of education and potentially more so. As you work out your own professional identity never let anyone get away with the 'working with young children is easy' argument, explicit or implied. It not only insults you, it also insults the children who you work with.

Moyles (2010, p.89) reminds us that not only is self-belief important for you from an internal perspective but also that 'educational improvement depends on practitioners feeling they WANT to make a difference; upon them feeling empowered and professional'. Traditional models of teacher efficacy and self-belief suggest that the early years of teaching are formative in this regard. For a Reception teacher efficacy does not arise only from the Early Years of teaching but from experience with every new class, from changing social and cultural pressures which shift over time and from a deeply rooted secure belief in your own practice. This book seeks to influence your sense of self-belief as a Reception teacher (that internal reassurance that you are doing a good job) and your self-efficacy (the capacity to believe in yourself and to advocate for what you do with confidence). Bandura (2005) created a teacher self-efficacy scale but for the authors of this book the measurement of self-efficacy is not particularly valuable or important. What is key for Reception teachers is to be able to reflect on what you do and why you do it, to sustain self-efficacy. Every teacher has had challenges and felt they could have done better; it takes strength of character to address these feelings and to come back again tomorrow. A secure image of yourself as a teacher can help you to do this.

The social construction of the teacher

Most people will nod with understanding when they are told someone is a teacher but the role of the teacher is seldom discussed. One widely chanted comment about teachers remains 'those who can do, those who can't teach'. This is unfair and off track to say the very least, but thinking of the Reception teacher most people who use the expression would be hard put to explain what it is that Reception teachers 'do'. Connell (2005, p.4) suggests there is an individual and collective 'knowing' in society in general about teachers, who they are and what they do. It seems teachers are in the public domain, to be talked about, to be praised and to be blamed, to be inspired by and to be turned off or demotivated by. Most people have a view of teachers because most of us have experienced being in education in one form or another. Teachers, teaching, education are among the things that people feel strongly about. The social and cultural constructivist idea of the teaching profession and of the 'teacher' and how individual teachers identify with this social construct as they become one is rather complex. In many people's minds the boundaries are blurred between social and personal identities as mentioned before. Rogoff (1990) discusses the social construction of the teacher and the learner. She highlights the socio-cultural construction of what it is to be a teacher; you work with children whose learning is both socially and culturally situated and consequently the identity of the teacher is socially and culturally constructed. One cannot be unpicked from the other and they are best seen as interwoven strands which are sometimes wound together tightly and sometimes less so. The culture of an individual school is set within the wider society in which it functions, and both have an impact on you as a Reception teacher.

So, as a Reception teacher, where do you fit in the public perception? Overarching ideas in society about teachers are not sufficiently nuanced to take account of the special nature of the Reception year. You are people who work with children who have left nursery or pre-school but are not yet in the world of the national curriculum, despite being on school premises.

Visit the hat shop

A simple image to capture some of the interchange between aspects of the Reception teacher's role is the 'hat shop'. Imagine yourself changing hats in line with the different parts of your role during the day, as the expectations and demands change. This is far more rapid than the pace of ecological transition proposed by Bronfenbrenner. You might wear a team leader's hat, a planner's hat and a nurse's hat before 9 a.m. By the end of the day, the week or the term the list of hats is long and varied and the Reception teacher often wears more than one hat at a time. So the hat shop has to be on the back burner to allow a serious consideration of what it means to be an aspirational Reception teacher.

Conclusion

In this chapter we have considered the 'facets of being' for a Reception teacher – re-examining theoretical concepts to construct a view about what it is to be a Reception teacher. Through examining the different identities of the Reception teacher and the roles they take in their professional lives an opportunity has been opened up for Reception teachers to find a voice and empower them to influence the social construction of the teaching role that is unique to this age group.

Reception teachers as a professional group share a distinctive ideology about children and about childhood. Being a member of that group makes you uniquely different from the larger group of school teachers as a whole. The Reception teacher's ideology is fed by a developmentally thorough understanding of children at age four. The next and pivotal chapter, Chapter 2, is about that very body of knowledge and understanding.

Being a member of the teaching profession is a rewarding role and a privilege. However, educating children cannot be solely the role of their teachers. It is often said that it takes a community to raise a child. Partnerships are essential to the shared endeavour. Children are entrusted to various members of the community at different stages of the child's life and the family's life. All of this contributes to shape the future for the child. This has to be set in the context of a credit model of the child as competent and capable. This behoves all who relate

Figure 1.3 Teacher and pupil take pleasure in learning together

to the child to stimulate and challenge them as they grow and change. Reception teachers are described in the UK as working in the 'Foundation Stage' and they hold a unique role in providing the secure foundations from which children flourish. The skills of lifelong learning are introduced in the Reception year, and the ingredients of a successful life, but it is the children themselves who will shape their futures. However much we cherish the children we teach, each is their own person and working with them at the wonderful age of four should be its own reward. As each class of children moves on new children will enter our lives and it is important to remain passionate about being a Reception teacher. Passion 'keeps the romance of teaching alive for great teachers' (Steinberg and Kincheloe, 1998, p.228).

The purpose of this chapter is not a sentimental one: it aims to provide each Reception teacher with ways of viewing their work and themselves. Thinking about the multiple identities you may hold as a Reception teacher can and should be liberating. It is a platform from which you can construct a personal professional identity, reflecting your values and beliefs.

Further inspiration

For a really interesting article (by a secondary school teacher) on parental and 'teacher' love, see http://www.sec-ed.co.uk/blog/is-professional-love-appropriate/ (last accessed January 2016).

For more on Hiram Powers, visit the website of the Smithsonian American Art Museum at http://americanart.si.edu/

References

Bandura, A. (2006) Adolescent development from an agentic perspective, in F. Pajares and T. Urdan (Eds) *Self-efficacy beliefs of adolescents*, (Vol. 5, pp.1–43). Greenwich, CT: Information Age Publishing.

Bronfenbrenner, U. (1979) *The ecology of human development.* Cambridge, MA: Harvard University Press.

Connell, R.W. (2005) *Masculinities (2nd ed.).* Cambridge: Polity Press.

Goldstein, L. (1998) More than gentle smiles and warm hugs: Applying the ethic of care to early childhood education. *Journal of Research in Childhood Education*, 12 (2): 244–62.

Griffin, A. (2008) 'Designer doctors': Professional identity and a portfolio career as a general practice educator. *Education for Primary Care*, 19: 355–9.

Hargreaves, A. (1994) *Changing teachers, changing times: Teachers' work and culture in the modern age.* London: Cassell.

Hargreaves, A. (1998) The emotional practice of teaching. *Teaching and Teacher Education,* 14 (8): 835–54.

Luff, P. and Kanyal, M. (2015) Maternal thinking and beyond: Towards a care-full pedagogy for early childhood. *Early Child Development and Care*, DOI:10.1080/03004430.2015.1028389.

Montessori, M. (1946) *Education for a new world.* Madras: Kalakshetra Publications.

Montessori, M. (1949/1992) *Education and peace* (H. Lane, Trans.). Oxford: Clio Press.

Moyles, J. (2010) Passion, paradox and professionalism in early years education. *Early Years. An International Journal of Research and Development,* 21 (2): 81–95.

Page, J. (2011) Do mothers want professional carers to love their babies? *Journal of Early Childhood Research,* 9 (3): 310–23.

Robinson, M. (2007) *Child development from birth to eight: A journey through the early years.* Maidenhead: Open University Press.

Rogoff, B. (1990) *Apprenticeship in thinking: Cognitive development in social context.* New York: Oxford University Press.

Rose, J. and Rogers, S. (2012) *The role of the adult in early years settings.* Maidenhead: Open University Press.

Steinberg, S. and Kincheloe, J. (1998) *Students as researchers –Creating classrooms that matter.* London: Falmer Press.

Jottings

2 Children at four

Eleonora Teszenyi

In this chapter we will begin to consider:

- what it means for children aged four to be 'ready' on the continuum of development;
- theory and research relating to child development;
- the five developmental areas – physical, cognitive, language, social and emotional.

Introduction

Reception teachers' multiple identities are predicated on their understanding of the children they are working with: who they are now, what brought them to this current stage of development and what experiences they have had prior to entering the Reception class. By law, children in England start school earlier than children in most of Europe. At four, most English children enter primary school; therefore, four is an age and stage that requires special attention and it is the focus of this chapter. There is much at stake. Children entering the Reception year may be just four or they can be turning five shortly after the start of the academic year. This one-year age gap can show up significant developmental differences between children. Unless the planned curriculum responds to the developmental characteristics of four- and five-year-old learners, our young children will not benefit as fully as they might from their early educational experience. The pedagogical approach to four year olds in a more formal environment, such as a school, requires serious consideration. To help Reception teachers value young children's early learning, some developmental characteristics of four year olds will be discussed next; particularly those that have important implications for practice.

In early childhood (UNESCO's 0–8 yrs range) all areas of development – social, emotional, language, cognitive, physical – are interconnected; they influence one another. For a child's healthy development, Reception teachers are expected to nurture all aspects of development in equal measure. This is through adopting an approach that is not only mindful but also 'care-full' (Luff and Kanyal, 2015, p.1748) of the whole child. The educational needs of four year olds are closely aligned with the developmental characteristics that they exhibit; therefore, effective Early Years pedagogies acknowledge practice that is developmentally appropriate. Educators who adopt a child-centred approach start with getting to know each individual child: their strengths, interests, backgrounds and family circumstances, their challenges. Home visits are wonderful for this. Staggered entry to school over a two- or three-week period also offers valuable opportunities for Reception teachers to talk to parents and carers of the children and find out about them too. A 'welcome box' containing a few significant items that portray the teacher themselves can help families get to know their children's Reception teacher so that an open, honest, reciprocal relationship can begin to develop. In this way they are able to support each child to grow and to learn in harmony with *who* they are rather than *what they can do* in relation to typical characteristics of developmental stages outlined in a curriculum document. In the same way that teachers have multiple identities (discussed in Chapter 1), children have, too. Their characteristics are unique and this uniqueness is much more than typical developmental traits. What really matters, what really is important to know about children can be found in the everyday nuances of children's lives. Attuned teachers can see, hear, feel and sense it as expressed by the hundred languages of children (Edwards et al., 1998): in their role play, in their dance or song, in their 2D/3D representations, through their behaviour, actions and through their talk.

The ever-expanding body of research on children's development over the last century provides an insight into the patterns and sequences of children's development. Children reach developmental milestones at different ages and their pace of development is unique to them. Close observations may reveal that some children 'dance' the developmental ladder and miss out phases in a sequence. This dance happens in partnership with supportive adults in an atmosphere of co-dependency. Some children may seem to plateau, while others display signs of accelerated development in a particular area. Rinaldi (2005, p.7) emphasises that learning and development are not linear; the journey is full of surprises, progress, 'standstills and retreats'. Our knowledge of children is, therefore, not linear either – more like a 'tangle of spaghetti' (Malaguzzi cited in Rinaldi, 2006, p.7). This complexity and the often-unexpected nature of development are what make teachers curious about each child. Understanding the developmental stage of four year olds provides Reception teachers with the foundation for professional decision making on experiences and learning opportunities that are not only developmentally and educationally relevant and meaningful for children but are also respectful of them. It is an essential part of being a highly skilled and competent Early Years teacher.

> ### Team talks and tasks
>
> Ask members of the team to reflect on how the development of their child or a child they know well was recorded. Can they think of a particular picture that captures a significant moment in that child's development? Why was this special to them? As a team, consider the ways in which you share examples of development with parents and carers.

Studying child development is not an exact science, there are no absolute truths. There are no formulas that, when applied, bring the same result every time. You only need to look at two children in the same family to know how uniquely different they are and to realise that what works for one child may not work for the other. The word 'development' in itself indicates this organic, fluid, ever-changing nature of children growing up.

Periods and principles of child development

It is useful to examine the periods and principles of child development before addressing some key aspects in the five areas of development, so that the implications for everyday practice, discussed later on in this chapter, are seen in a meaningful context.

> ### Point to ponder
>
> The distinct periods of development are identified as *prenatal* – from conception to birth; *infancy and toddlerhood* – from birth to 2 years; *early childhood* – from 2 to 6 years; *middle childhood* – from 6 to 11; and *adolescence* – from 11 to 18 years (Berk, 2006). Make a note or use the blank Jottings page at the end of the chapter to record some of what you know about each stage.

Reception age children fall within the period of *early childhood,* which, in broad terms, is characterised by more self-control and self-sufficiency. Children physically become longer and leaner, their motor skills become more refined and make-believe play dominates, supporting many aspects of social and emotional development. Language develops and vocabulary expands at a remarkable rate and children position, even assert, themselves in the social world of their peers and family. It is also important to remember that the age of four is within the period of the most rapid growth between birth and approximately seven, at which point development starts to slow down (Fisher, 2013). This window from birth to seven in development is crucial and referred to as the formative years, laying the foundations for lifelong learning. The stage of development at four is part of this continuum, has its own characteristics, derives from past experiences and links to future development. Young children in Reception classes of primary schools are not immature, as sometimes believed by some; they are just being four (Cleave and Brown, 1993).

The principles of development listed below are adapted from Feeney et al. (2013) and they aim to underpin Reception teachers' desire to plan an appropriate Early Years curriculum where the 'appropriateness' is firmly rooted in developmental understanding.

Development is holistic: all areas are interlinked and interconnected. It is only for close study that we break up development into its components –to gain a more in-depth knowledge of the individual areas that make up the whole. Imagine a group of children trying to find a solution to getting to the treasure box key that is frozen inside a block of ice. Trying and testing out ideas provides evidence for cognitive functions, their discussions and debates reflect language development, children working together towards a shared aim supports social development and when some equipment is used to dislodge that key, they are developing physically, too. The development of one area would not happen without the development of another.

Development follows predictable patterns: This implies a steady predictable progress with milestones reached in a particular sequence throughout childhood. It is assumed to be continual and cumulative but is also characterised by some plasticity. Bruce and Meggitt (2003, p.60) consider it more of a 'network'. For example, a child may return from foreign travel where the handling of larger notes of currency triggers an interest and the development of the mathematical (or cognitive) skill of counting in tens or hundreds before mastering counting by rote to 20. This may seem like a side step (as in the dance metaphor earlier) from what is deemed to be 'normal' mathematical development but the awareness and understanding of tens and hundreds add to the network of mathematical skills, which strengthens the concept of quantity and the ability to count progressively larger amounts.

Rates of development vary: Ages and stages refer to two distinct things – age is the child's biological age and stage is a phase of development the child is displaying typical signs of at a given time. The direction of development is similar for all children but the pace varies greatly – children develop at their own rate. There has to be a warning around the use of normative measures when determining children's stages of development against their biological age; they can be used to label children as forward or backward. Mothers often compare ages at which their children start to walk. It is perfectly normal for children to gain control over gravity, stand up and take a few steps between the ages of 9 and 17 months (Bayley, 2005). A child starting to walk at 9 months cannot be regarded as forward in the same vein as a child making those first few steps at the age of 17 months cannot be labelled as backward. Normative measures or developmental milestones are designed to outline the curve of development (the typical sequence of skills) to help make professional judgements.

Development is influenced by experience: In the 'heredity versus experience' or 'nature versus nurture' debate, nature refers to the biological make-up of children, the genetically determined process of maturation. Nurture encompasses the experiences children have after they are born in the process of growing up. The earlier reinforces a scientific view of child development whereas the latter acknowledges the social nature of development. The debate is ongoing, there is no definitive or conclusive understanding of the extent nature and nurture impact on the different areas of child development. It is the unique interaction between heredity and experience that influences human development on an individual basis. For example, it is often noted that children who have access to a language-rich environment show signs of accelerated language and literacy development compared to those children who lack opportunities to converse and communicate with others.

Development is influenced by culture: Development cannot be understood outside a cultural, historical context (Penn, 2005). Children grow up in a 'unique combination of genetic and environmental circumstances' that can result in different paths of development (Berk, 2006, p.8) because cultural values and beliefs determine what experiences children are offered throughout childhood. For example, children in nomadic countries where families follow their herds develop spatial concepts, spatial awareness, mapping ability and sense of orientation/direction earlier and to a more advanced degree. Home visits provide an insight to the experiences children whom you teach have access to, as determined by the home culture.

What comes next in our journey into child development?

Looking at the development typical at the age of four for all the areas of child development is beyond the bounds of this one single chapter. Instead, some aspects of each developmental area will be addressed; the aspects that have implications for everyday practice, the ones that are probably the most discussed among Reception teachers. Within the area of physical development key categories of fundamental movement skills, fine manipulation in relation to handwriting, balance and proprioception will be addressed. To help support Reception teachers' understanding of social development the issues of friendships, children's peer culture, the skills of self-organisation and self-esteem will be discussed. The cognitive development section addresses deep level learning and thinking, the development of the brain and its capability for cognitive tasks. In relation to emotional development, the focus will be on intrinsic versus external rewards and emotional regulation. Finally, language development will address the significance of a language-rich environment, the strands and components of language including non-verbal communication and the skill of listening. Theories around these selected aspects of child development will be drawn on to help identify the whys and hows of effective Early Years practice.

Physical development

This is the most visible, most observable, but at the same time the most discrete aspect of human development. Typical characteristics of a four-year-old child are:

- Growth is not as rapid as in infancy but there is still steady increase in weight, height and muscles mass (Gallahue and Ozmun, 2006).

- Body proportions change significantly in early childhood: the chest becomes larger than the abdomen and the stomach flattens significantly.

- Senses are still developing; eye balls don't reach their full size till the age of 12, so young children tend to be farsighted. This means they are not ready for extended periods of close work. They have more taste buds than adults and because of the shortness of the Eustachian tube (connecting the middle ear with the throat) children are more prone to ear infections which affects their hearing (Gallahue and Ozmun, 2006).

- Children at four and five rapidly develop a variety of stability and motor skills but they are still more comfortable with unilateral (hopping, galloping) than bilateral (skipping) movement. They are energetic (would rather run than walk) and need ample space to be able to explore with their bodies through movement. 'The timid, cautious and measured movements of the 2 to 3 year old gradually give way to the confident, eager, and often reckless abandon of the 4 and 5 year olds' (Gallahue and Ozmun, 2006, p.176). They also need short but frequent rest periods to recharge batteries because of the intensity with which Reception age children play and work.

- Fine motor control is not fully established yet because of the proximo-distal direction of development and of the wide gaps between the wrist bones; the gaps fill in almost fully by six and a half and completely fused by the age of 14 and a half. Girls are considerably ahead of boys in this (adapted from Berk, 2006).

Gallahue and Ozmun (1998, p.3) acknowledge the roles of both nature and nurture when they define motor development as 'continuous change in motor behaviour throughout the life cycle, brought about by interaction among the requirements of the task, the biology of the individual, and the conditions of the environment'. According to their staged development theory, Reception age children fall in the *fundamental movement* phase (which is typical for children between two and seven) and within this phase, four to five year olds are at an *elementary stage* of physical development (between the *initial stage* of two to three year olds and the *mature stage* of six to seven year olds). The elementary stage is characterised by increased exploration of movement capabilities where improved co-ordination is evident along with the improved synchronisation of spatial and temporal elements; temporal meaning 'the time series in which the movement occurs' (Gallahue and Ozmun, 2006, p.17). Gallahue and Ozmun (1998) helpfully identify three primary categories of fundamental movements, which help Reception teachers to understand and plan physical activities which support a broad and balanced PE curriculum stretching beyond the more limited view of supporting children to develop their fine and gross motor skills only. These are: *stability, locomotion and manipulation* (both fine and gross). *Stability* they define as 'gaining and maintaining one's equilibrium in relation to the force of gravity' (p.80), which translates to movements such as twisting, turning, pushing and pulling. *Locomotion* refers to children changing location of their bodies and moving through space which manifests itself in walking, running, jumping, hopping, skipping or leaping, for example. The familiar term of *manipulation* straddles both fine and gross manipulation. Gross manipulation or gross motor skills encompass 'imparting force to or receiving force from objects' (p.80), such as throwing, catching, kicking, striking. Fine manipulation or fine motor skills refer to the 'intricate use of the muscles of the hand and wrist' (p.80), for example: sawing, cutting, threading, pinching, drawing and writing. Gross manipulation precedes fine manipulation because of the proximo-distal direction of development (Berk, 2006). Motor control develops from the proximal (close to the body) to the distal (further from the centre of the body). Core stability and the control of movement from the shoulders and arms come before controlling the movement of the wrists. Therefore, to engage in fine motor tasks often associated with literacy, such as handwriting, would be unreasonable to expect of a child before having the opportunities to develop their gross motor skills through energetic, large-scale activities. The fundamental movement abilities are first mastered separately by the child then they are combined and further developed to become specific sport skills later on; for example, when children do skipping with a rope, play bat and ball or kick the ball in football. Each skill is the product of earlier motor attainments and forms the foundation for new skills.

Mastering these fundamental movement skills separately first has implications for practice. Providing opportunities for outdoor play puts four- to five-year-old children at a distinct advantage because the outdoors (discussed in Chapter 6) facilitates large-scale movement through active discovery, which in return stretches movement boundaries. Maude (2001) applies the familiar term of 'literacy' to physical development and advocates that teachers help children acquire *movement vocabulary* by providing plenty of opportunities to explore through movement in a great variety of situations. With repetition, these fundamental movement skills are registered in *movement memory*. Refinement through regular practice improves efficiency and mastery of actions, which results in *movement quality*. One-off activities and opportunities to develop high quality physical skills are not sufficient. Children will not develop their balance by including the balancing beams in one or two PE sessions. As with everything else, children need opportunities to revisit experiences and practise, so setting up an environment (the continuous provision) that allows this is crucial. This is explored in more detail in Chapter 5. Children need to have regular access to benches and beams, lines and carefully placed logs or tyres to balance on. In this way, Reception teachers make a real contribution to teaching children 'to appreciate their bodies and the wondrous things they can do' (Martens, 1978, p.15).

Figure 2.2a and b Expanding movement boundaries for physical development

Handwriting

I would like to return to handwriting at the age of four and the developmental appropriateness or inappropriateness of it, as it tends to be a key feature of Reception children's daily lives at school. As mentioned above, at the age of four the bone structure of the wrist is not sufficiently developed to exercise precise control over writing implements such as pencils on a small scale. The gaps between the wrist bones account for the slower and gradual development of fine manipulation. In the palmer or power grip, where the entire hand is used for grasping and holding the pencil, children control the movement through their shoulder and arm, therefore the movement is larger. At a closer look, you may see some children use these larger and less controlled movements when colouring in pictures, therefore pencil marks go outside the outline of an image. A pincer grip assumes greater control of the writing implement. The pencil is held between the finger(s) and the thumb and the source of the more precise movement is the muscles in the fingers and wrist. The control is greater, resulting in smaller movement, consequently in smaller writing. When the movement is controlled by the muscles in the wrist, colouring becomes neater and stays within the lines. The development of the muscles responsible for fine movement can be a long and sometimes painful process. Reception teachers may see children dropping their pencils or scissors and shaking their hands to relax their muscles off after a longer bout of writing or cutting; very much same way as runners shake their legs out after a long run or a fast sprint. Activities that help develop the strength of the muscles in the hand provide children with effective support: moulding clay and playdough, finger rhymes, sculpting wet sand and soil, using water pistols and pegs.

Proprioception

One key element of stability, identified as one of the three categories of movement by Gallahue and Ozmun (1998), is balance. Secure balance is directly linked to postural control, which depends on the maturity of the proprioceptive system. Proprioception derives from the Latin *'proprius'*, meaning 'one's own' and refers to 'the knowledge of the inner self' (Goddard-Blythe, 2005, p.16). It is the sense of body parts in relation to one another. This knowledge or sense is gained through movement experiences and the maturation of the vestibular system, which takes at least seven years and continues in puberty and beyond. The vestibular system is the sensory system that provides a sense of balance and orientation in space to co-ordinate movement. Immature vestibular functioning can often be the cause of learning difficulties such as dyslexia, dyspraxia or attention problems (Goddard-Blythe, 2005). Children's knowing their own position in space is crucial to spatial and directional awareness and orientation, which are the foundations of some cognitive functions such as reading and writing or the concept of time, for example. In English we write and read from left to right. Distinguishing between the two and understanding 'up' and 'down' is required for handwriting, awareness of 'before' and 'after' helps children tell the time. Learning to develop directional awareness is underpinned by knowing your own position in space. Children cannot be expected to form a line/circle or walk in a line unless their proprioception is mature enough to locate themselves in space that is static and/or dynamic. Reversing letters, numbers or words after the age of eight can often be traced back to immature vestibular system and balance (Goddard-Blythe, 2005). Reception teachers can help children develop or train their balance by planning activities that require changes of movement in space: trampolining, bouncy castles, going down slides, swinging, dancing, mapping and tracking or exploring the centrifugal forces of carousels, spinning, rolling down the hill and so on. What fun this learning can be. Children who seem to be clumsy, dropping things and knocking things over, who have difficulties in copying movements or understanding personal space (going too close to people and having collisions), those who find learning to ride a bike difficult or those who have no fear or excessive fear of heights would benefit from these activities and movement opportunities.

Point to ponder

If proprioception is still developing, why are we asking children to move from one place to another in a line? And why do we get upset when they cannot do it? How does the rule 'sitting down and facing forward' on a slide impact on the boundaries of exploration of movement? How can you provide children with opportunities to develop all three primary categories of movement: stability, locomotion and manipulation?

Cognitive development

This refers to the development of thinking, concepts, mental representations, the workings and processes of the mind that lead to understanding and making sense of the world. While a relationship between cognitive and motor development has been suggested and debated on the premise that healthy physical development is a pre-requisite for learning and cognitive functions (Diamond, 2002; Anderson, 2002; Wassenberg et al., 2005), it is now uncontested that play saturates young children's lives in early childhood (two to six years) and it is the primary mode through which they learn about their capabilities. Brown (2008) claims that play activates the neural networks of the brain like no other human activity does. He advocates *object play* where the hand and the brain are connected through the exploration and manipulation of objects that the child is playing with. The same notion is pertinently expressed by Malaguzzi (cited in Edwards et al., 1998, p.3) asserting that adults cannot expect children to 'think without hands, to do without head'. Play facilitates cognitive growth and a four year old is typically characterised by:

- mentally (as well as physically) being active, mastering a wide range of skills and competencies through hands-on exploration;

- experimenting with the concrete, rather than the abstract as he is making sense of the world. Beginning to hypothesise through trial and error in problem solving. He needs to see that there are a variety of ways of doing things, not just one way, the 'right' way;

- increased ability to express ideas and thoughts. These are in the present so he needs to do things NOW and talk about it while he is engaged. He is curious and needs to ask questions;

- imagination and fantasy drive action;

- shows preference in learning styles, learns at own pace and expresses interests (sometimes the fascination can be obsessive)(adapted from Berk, 2006).

Playing with objects takes the child through a sequence of exploration. First the child asks: 'what is this?'; next he wonders: 'what can this do?'; and finally the boundaries of exploration stretch and the child seeks to find out: 'what can I do with this?' This has implications for Reception teachers seeking to understand children in observation as well as when teaching. When observing children, it is useful to establish how the child is exploring in his play: is he at the stage of examining what the object is or is he now studying what the object does? More complex cognitive processing takes place when a child starts to experiment with the object to find out what he can do with it. Unusual objects or ordinary objects in unusual situations provoke children's curiosity and desire to find out. A dog collar at the end of a lead hanging on a tree branch in the garden can result in children being deeply involved in seeking out who the collar belongs to and how it got there. Ideas could flow, suggestions could lead to hypothesis then to action and enthusiastic children won't rest till they find an explanation.

Figure 2.3 Cognitive learning

These provocations for learning (addressed again in Chapter 5) engage children in deep-level learning, as opposed to the surface-level learning they experience through instructional activities (mainly adult-led), which offer children significantly less opportunities to think for themselves. This superficial learning 'does not affect the basic competencies of the child' (Laevers, 2006, p.21) and because learning can often be out of context, the child cannot transfer the learnt skills to real life situations as easily. Deep-level learning requires active involvement from the child with hands on and brain switched on. This type of involvement is characterised by curiosity and an exploratory drive, which, as Laevers (2006) points out, brings the child and the adult into the most intense form of concentration and guarantees lifelong learning.

Point to ponder

Katz (cited in House 2011, p.128) suggests that 'uncovering' rather than 'covering' a subject in the planned curriculum is more conducive to deep-level learning and steers Reception teachers away from content-based teaching. Find out more about Lillian Katz, you could jot down some of her wisdom in the Jottings space at the end of the chapter.

Imagination and creativity are key components of thinking and cognition and four year olds have them in abundance. It is the Reception teachers' role to respect, recognise and nurture creativity in children's everyday play and facilitate it in a way that allows free flow of original ideas and new meanings. Open-ended resources and the open-endedness of activities and experiences support this well. An art workshop can be created where a broad range of resources are presented in an aesthetically pleasing way with unlimited access throughout the day. Children can then choose what they want and need to express themselves in their own way.

> ## ? Point to ponder
>
> Have you ever wondered why some children don't access junk modelling? What does this term suggest? How much value do we (and they) attribute to 'junk'? Would children be more tempted to use recycled materials if they were organised and sorted into clearly labelled containers for easy navigation?

In the graphics/mark making area children could draw and write on potatoes, oranges, lemons or even blown-up balloons (3D rather than 2D surfaces). These items don't need to stay in that specific area – they can be transferred to the home corner with the written 'messages' to be interpreted and further developed. When presenting the ingredients for a cooking activity, for example, why not swap one egg in the egg box with a truly life-like rubber egg that has been sprayed with gold paint? Imagine the children's faces when they open the lid of the egg box. How would this provocation inspire them to use their imagination and creativity?

This open-endedness also applies to the teaching strategies that Reception teachers employ when supporting young children's learning. Questioning is one of the main strategies used to scaffold children's learning, however, *suggesting* ('You might like to try…'), *re-capping* ('So far you have …'), *reciprocating* ('You were right in wearing gloves for building the snowman. My hands are freezing.'), *inviting to elaborate* ('I really want to know more about…'), *clarifying* ('Ok, so you think that…') and *offering own experience* ('When I last cut a rotten apple in half…') may prove equally useful strategies to encourage creative and critical thinking (adapted from Dowling, 2010). Open-ended questions are designed to offer children opportunities to think of a variety of answers, as opposed to give the one right answer. But are all questions used by Reception teachers open ended? For example: Where does flour come from? Most teachers would know the answer to this; therefore, they expect the correct answer of 'ground from wheat'. A truly open-ended question is one that neither the teacher, nor the child knows the answer to. 'Who does this odd collection of clothing in this suitcase belong to? Why was it left here?' These types of questions sustain shared critical thinking and afford real problem-solving opportunities.

To conclude this cognitive development section, let us look more closely at the development of the brain and how it functions at the age of four. The human brain has 100 to 200 billion neurons (nerve cells), which create a neural network by connecting to one another. The greatest number of connections (synapses) is formed within the first three years of a child's life, followed by synaptic pruning to form more stable neural networks. Brain cells that are seldom stimulated lose their connections; they are cut out from the network – 40 per cent of synapses are pruned throughout childhood (Oates et al., 2012). When the brain does this 'spring clean', children may be less focused and more fractious; they may appear like four-year-old boys at the time of the testosterone rush. The large bundle of nerves connecting the two hemispheres of the brain is called the corpus callosum, which integrates aspects of thinking such as attention, perception, problem solving, memory and language by securing cross-talk between the two sides of the brain. The more complex the task, the more important this cross-talk is between the two hemispheres. The production of neural connections of the corpus callosum peaks between the ages of three and six (Thompson et al., 2000). As the brain develops, children complete more and more complex cognitive tasks but four year olds' biologically immature capacities cannot be seen as deficit; instead, implications for practice must be considered. Children need to be offered challenging tasks that are developmentally appropriate and allow them to think in concrete as opposed to abstract terms. Overly complex stimulation may result in overwhelming the brain's neural circuits. It is crucially important to remember that between the ages of two and six children's brainwaves begin to speed up from Delta (0.5–3 Hertz, dominating an infant's brain), to Theta (4–8 Hertz), which feeds on rich imagination, fantasy and creativity at this age. This frequency, however, is not the most efficient to process complex cognitive tasks, such as addition doubles, number bonds to 10, or subtraction, particularly when taught in the abstract. From around the age of six, the brain wave frequency further increases to Alpha (8–12 Hertz), which allows more accelerated learning and more complex connections between ideas and concepts to be made (Goddard-Blythe, 2005). This coincides with Piaget's (1952) concrete operational stage of development (between the ages of seven and eleven) as well as the beginning of Key Stage 1 in England. The Piagetian concrete operational stage is characterised by logical, flexible and organised thinking, when the concepts of conservation, serration, classification, spatial reasoning, etc. develop. Make-believe play (which is excellent for the development of mental representations), sensory and movement play help the process of acceleration of the brain waves, therefore presenting children with activities in several sensory and motor modalities is essential for development at this stage.

Point to ponder

Could there be a link between understanding how children's brains develop and determining school starting ages?

Language development

Mastering proficiency in verbal language is of one the most significant milestones not only in development in general but also in children's cognitive development (Vygotsky, 1978; Bruner, 1983). It is a tool for organising knowledge, connecting ideas and making thinking visible (or should I say audible). Language is defined as an organised system of symbols to communicate verbally or non-verbally with others (Doherty and Hughes, 2014). The development of young children's linguistic ability is significantly influenced by early experiences of interaction and talk with people.

The rate at which language develops in the first two years of life is extraordinary, and by the age of four children's language development can typically be described like this:

- Vocabulary increases to 1000 words.

- Starting to use more complex sentences, which are similar to what adults use.

- Beginning to understand formal rules of grammar but generalisation of those rules still occur (i.e. 'foots' instead of 'feet' used for plural).

- Tenses are present: past, present and future are used – again, overgeneralisation of rules result in incorrect use of irregular past tense (i.e. 'runned' instead of 'ran').

- Uses prepositions (after, with, for, etc.), negatives (no/not, -less, dis-) and imperatives (for exclamation and command); double negative is also used: 'I didn't bring no packed lunch'.

- Increasingly asking more 'why' questions.

- Uses language for conversation and for narrative – better at conversations on a one-to-one basis rather than in larger groups; still tends to interrupt and talk simultaneously.

- Critical listening skills are lacking: children's understanding of what is said is very literal (you may find children taking a paint pot outside to paint on the flowers if the instruction was: 'We are going to paint those flowers today.').

- Manipulates language effectively through rhymes and riddles and metaphors.

- By the end of Reception, children adjust their language to the listener and the context.

(Doherty and Hughes, 2014)

The National Literacy Trust (2005) and Bercow (2008) report that children's communication skills are declining and their speaking and listening skills deteriorating. This alarming trend can be attributed to a number of life-style factors: changing work patterns of parents (which leaves less time for talk with their children); a reduction in shared family mealtimes (which means less time for conversation); playing with parents being replaced by long periods of watching TV or playing on mobile technologies (which reduces opportunities for social engagements and talk); constant background noise (which reduces children's listening abilities). Based on their research findings, Hart and Risley (2003) suggest that at the age of four an average child in a professional family would experience almost 45 million words, an average child in a working-class family 26 million words, and an average child in a family of socio-economic disadvantage 13 million words. This gap of over 30 million by the age of four has implications for practice in a Reception class, making teachers seriously think about the language experiences they provide for children. Understanding language development, which goes beyond the realms of vocabulary and the use of grammatically correct sentences, therefore, helps Reception teachers offer a comprehensive language-rich environment because they consider all four key components and the three strands of language.

A distinct alignment can be made between the key components and strands of language: the strand *speech*, which refers to the child's ability to articulate sounds, aligns with the key component of phonology (the sounds of language). The second strand, *language*, is connected with semantics (which is the combination of words that create different meaning) and grammar (the rules of putting words together to express intended and unambiguous meaning). Finally, the fourth key component, pragmatics (which is the conventions of

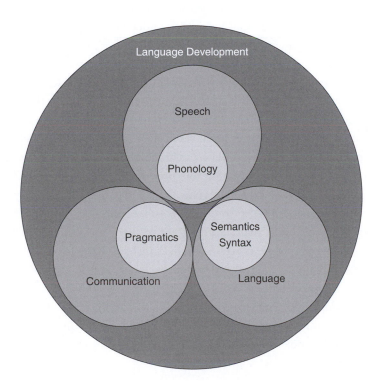

Figure 2.1 The interlinking elements of language development

how to use language in different contexts), aligns with the third strand of language: *communication,* referring to the ability to use language to express meaning. With this in-depth understanding, a Reception teacher can plan activities, experiences and adjust his/her own interactions to individual children so that every aspect of language can be nurtured. This forms the foundations for literacy, for developing the skills of reading, writing and comprehension.

According to Argyle (1994) 93 per cent of our communication is non-verbal so decoding non-verbal clues is equally important when engaging with others. Reception teachers' understanding of the non-verbal forms of communication gives depth to their dialogue and talk with children. This is particularly important in the Early Years when children often use non-verbal forms of communication (for example: they express joy in their dance, agitation in the way they beat the drum, lack of trust as they position themselves in the environment in a way that allows them to keep an eye on all the goings-on). The non-verbal forms of communication are helpfully identified by Graddol et al. (1994) as: gestures, body contact (handshake, hug, touch), posture, personal space and distance between people, gaze/eye contact (being the richest form of non-verbal communication) and facial expression (e.g. frown, wink, baring teeth). Sometimes, non-verbal clues speak volumes and sensitive adults not only ascribe meaning to them skilfully but also consider them with equal significance. However, this requires advanced skills in listening. It may be useful to draw on what Rinaldi (2005, p.17) calls the 'pedagogy of listening and relationships' to understand the depth and breadth of this concept. 'Listening' is often distinguished from 'active listening', which is a technique used in counselling where the listener re-states what was said to confirm his/her understanding. This is still a mechanical process compared to how Rinaldi (ibid.) defines 'listening' in its multiple layers. She draws attention to the significance of adults being sensitive to the patterns that connect children and teachers with one another in a classroom. Openness to listen and to be listened to with all of the senses helps us understand the hundred languages of children. The importance of time is acknowledged but not in a chronological sense; rather, with reference to 'interior time' (p.20) that allows for a comfortable pace of life, for pauses and silences, for just being. Listening is an emotional labour that generates doubt, interest, curiosity, desire and above all: love. Listening enables Reception teachers to recognise the value of the differences in children's perspectives of things that are important to them. A highly skilled listener is able to suspend judgements and prejudices and reflect instead. Reflection is the premise of any learning relationship and through listening one '*re-knows*' and '*re-cognises*' (p.21) theories, ideas; the act of which consequently gives an individual visibility in a community of learners, lifts one out of anonymity. The child's and the adult's ability to listen and to be listened to is what enables effective communication and meaningful dialogue (as opposed to monologue) in reciprocal and inter-dependent relationships. A Reception class should be a 'context of multiple listening' (p.22).

> **? Point to ponder**
>
> How can you support the development and the strengthening of the articulatory system: lips, mouth, tongue, vocal cords? What evidence can you see of the different components of effective listening in the classroom?

Social development

Children are social beings, they are born with a social brain (Gopnik et al., 2001), they want to be involved, they want to be part of a group and much of their learning takes place in a social context. The stage of *social development* at the age of four is typically characterised by:

- playing as individuals but becoming increasingly aware of others, seeking out interactions. Learning to share and work together. More comfortable in small groups or pairs than in large groups;

- establishing self-identity; by the age of three most children are able to label their own and other's sex (boy or girl) and around four gender stability starts to develop: girls recognise that they will grow up to be mummies, boys will become daddies. They become more increasingly aware that change of clothing and hairstyle does not necessarily change one's sex. Gender stereotyping occurs and strengthens. Ethnic identity starts to develop;

- self-esteem that is typically high but also frail as children start to make comparisons based on responses from others;

- recognition that they and other people can have different feelings and ideas but they may still confuse the two (was it my idea or my peer's?);

- beginning to show sensitivity to other's intentions when making moral judgements (what is right or wrong), displays morally relevant behaviours;

- having an understanding of authority figures;

- friendships continuing to develop, mainly manifesting themselves in engaging in shared make-believe and common activities; there is also an emotional quality to it, offering support for each other (crucial at times of transitions). This concern for each other will lead to loyalty later on (adapted from Berk, 2006).

Four-year-old children actively participate in their own socialisation. They strive to take control of their own lives and they also want to share that control with others.

This participation and sharing is what makes up children's peer cultures. For us to study and to understand this culture from the children's perspectives, we need to move from our adult world, leave behind our often-preconceived ideas and get behind the scenes of young children's social lives.

Friendship is one of the key components of children's social world; they are the first close relationships after family relations and signify a new form of independence from parents. It is a reciprocal relationship that goes beyond acceptance and popularity – which are one-way constructs (Dunn, 2004). Reception teachers must look beyond what may appear as friendship on the surface. Children being friends one day but not the other, falling out easily, reflect how they gradually and reassuringly acquire social competence, empathy and an understanding of socially acceptable forms of behaviour in line with their evolving capabilities. Friendship matters to children. When Reception teachers separate friends because they are considered as disruptive or mischievous together, valuable social learning opportunities are taken away from them. Managing and maintaining friendships are complex tasks. Adults can suspend dialogue or interactions with friends easily enough and they are able to pick up again once disruptions are handled. For four year olds, this is a more challenging task not only because they are still developing social skills but also because they may not have the language and cognitive skills to manage complex social interactions yet. For young children, those who they are playing with are friends, and those who they are not are threats to friendship, and they would go a long way to protect their interactive space. 'In fact, they are not refusing to share, rather they want to keep sharing what they are already sharing' (Corsaro, 2003, p. 40). Children who enter a group's play uninvited are taking a significant social risk and are likely to get rejected or resisted. Children need opportunities to take social risks as much as physical risks so they learn about their own social capabilities. Although Reception teachers may refrain from interfering with disputes and leave the children to sort the issue out among themselves, it is equally important to protect children from emotional (and sometimes physical) abuse from peers. It can prove to be an effective strategy to remind children wanting to enter others' play that their desire to join in may be quite different from the others, who want to keep the play intact amongst themselves. However, if this happens often and goes unnoticed by the teachers, it could lead to children becoming disrespectful of their peers and a 'you can't play here' culture could develop. For children to live and play harmoniously with each other in a community of learners, learning some effective access strategies are crucial. Often, the first step is 'nonverbal entry' (Corsaro, 2003, p.42), when a child places himself in the area where the play is taking place and observes the activity. Parten (1932) referred to this as 'onlooker' play and it is typically associated with timidity, although it is not necessarily this. However, when children are attempting to enter others' play, this may be part of a complex set of behaviours that secures access to play. It is often followed by the child doing something similar to what the others are doing in their play and it can also go with private speech (Vygotsy, 1978): the child narrating his own actions. Children are afraid that others coming along would upset the sharing that they have already achieved. Direct bids for entry such as 'What are you doing?' or

'Can I play?' often indicate that the child wanting to enter the play does not know what the play is about, what has happened so far and where the play is going; therefore, the entry would cause trouble. Reception teachers can help children learn effective entry strategies by talking to them in different play scenarios and by modelling entry themselves.

However, getting inside the children's play is not an easy task for adults. Children's relationships with peers are on a horizontal plane, whereas their relationships with adults are of a vertical nature, where children are seen as less powerful (Hartup, 1989). What Corsaro (2003, p.10) calls 'reactive entry strategy' seems to be one of the most respectful ways of Reception teachers involving themselves in children's play. Similarly to the access strategy described above for children, teachers' entry to established play also starts with the non-verbal entry. It continues with playing parallel and along the theme of the observed play until children address the teacher verbally or non-verbally; sometimes adults are handed play equipment as if to say 'you can join in now'. This is when teachers react to the invitation and enter children's play. Once 'inside', great care should be taken that the adult does not start to dominate the play but follows the roles allocated by the children and contributes within the parameters that the children have set. Being accepted in play situations affords an opportunity to truly understand what children's friendships are like and helps Reception teachers resist the temptation to separate friends. Instead, they can learn to respect the friendship that travels on rocky roads with its ups and downs.

Point to ponder

Is it always appropriate to share toys and equipment or even share out roles in children's play?

Protecting interactive space is more dominant in newly formed communities of children/ learners. Would children and teachers/TAs benefit from staying together as a group over a longer period of time? Would this support group dynamics to settle and work effectively on an even keel? Is transitioning from one teacher to another, from one classroom to another, necessary each year? Is it in the children's interest or is it an organisational imperative? Something that we have always done in schools, an idea that we are too wedded to?

Another facet of social development that has significant implications for practice is children's skills and ability of self-organisation (or lack of it). Some children may have difficulties in living and playing harmoniously with their peers in a Reception class or they find it hard to use the environment and resources in the way that is designed to facilitate learning. This could be because children may not have developed the competence of self-organisation. Laevers (2006) identifies four key components to developing self-organisational skills and the ability to follow codes of conduct established by a community of learners (children and teachers alike). They are:

1. the will to commit to an activity or play experience;

2. the ability to make choices, to decide what to do;

3. the ability to recreate, revisit play scenarios and to develop them further;

4. to assess the play or activity in view of what the child set out to achieve.

Self-organisation is the pre-cursor for developing a play ethic, learning ethic and, later on, work ethic. Laevers (2006, p.22) emphasises that self-organisational skills are essential for lifelong learning, fundamental to the 'art of living' and they are particularly powerful when combined with creativity.

? Point to ponder

How can Reception teachers support the development of self-organisational skills in the classroom? What kind of investments do they need to make? When is the best time?

A final key issue of social development discussed in this section is four-year-old children's self-esteem. Children at this age are often heard proudly saying that they are the best at many things (the fastest or the strongest, for example), which evidences self-esteem being high as claimed by developmental research. The reason for this is that children at this stage of social development perceive their desired abilities as their actual abilities, they do not differentiate between the two. This leaves them rather vulnerable and their high self-esteem frail. With a sensitive approach and thoughtful responses a Reception teacher can support children with learning to see their abilities in a more realistic light. Bringing the 'desired' and 'actual' together is also supported by their developing understanding of social referencing, which enables children to see themselves as they are perceived by others, through the responses and reactions they receive. The two small vignettes exemplify this crucially significant aspect of social development.

Vignette

Callum is very interested in sport and physical activity and he regularly watches Sportacus *on the cbeebies channel on television. He is a four-year-old boy who would be described as a reluctant writer. He is in the writing area and completely absorbed in drawing an image of his hero. Once the picture of Sportacus is done, he decides to add some captions, which offer advice on how to get fit. In his emergent writing, some very deliberate large-scale marks are made, he writes from left to right and*

*the letter shapes 'j'(for the word 'jump' in 'star jump') and 'u' (for 'up' in 'press up') are recognis-
able. Once he is finished, he takes his drawing to his Reception teacher, shows it to her and reads out
the captions. The Reception teacher recognises Sportacus immediately, she praises the accuracy of the
image and with an appreciative tone she points out the letter shapes that are recognisable in Callum's
writing. The teacher concludes her comments with: 'I'm very pleased with this. You are a good little
writer, Callum'. He looks at the teacher with disbelieving eyes and says 'Oh, not me; that's Olivia!'*

Vignette

*Joe is completing a task set by his peers: he is designing and writing a sign for the role-play area
that they are setting up. The large rectangular sign is decorated with strings of ivy brought in from
the woodland area of the school playground and it says: 'the giants cassul'. He is beaming with pride
as he brings the sign to the role-play area to be fixed on the dividing boards. The Reception teacher
thanks him and says: 'You are very good at this, Joe! Well done'. He then responds with a broad smile
and a quick twirl with his arms stretched high up: 'Don't well-done me, I know I am good at this'.
Then he skips off.*

Points to ponder

What do the two vignettes tell us about possible previous comments and
responses to these two boys? How have they come to these two very
different conclusions about their abilities and what lessons can we learn from the
two incidents? How does organising children into ability groups in a Reception class
support or hinder self-esteem at this tender age?

Emotional development

While understanding children's cognitive development helps to understand how well
they may comprehend what is asked of them, an **emotional** attunement helps to predict
how children might respond. Emotions are the 'powerhouse for shaping and determining
our mental well-being and framing the way we behave, interact and live alongside others'
(Robinson, 2009, p.30). Through expressing feelings of joy, pleasure, happiness, fear or
sadness, children maintain social relationships and friendships, which allow for mutual
care and concern to develop. Four year olds' emotional development can be described
as follows:

- They are less stable than five year olds and more at the mercy of their changing moods, fears and emotional outbursts. They are aware of their emotions but need adult support to verbalise them.

- Less dependent on an adult but still requiring security in the form of attachments to key persons both at home and at school.

- They require predictability of care and a regular and familiar pattern to the day with flexibility and freedom of choice in how they can achieve their goals.

- Learning to regulate their behaviour and emotions, still requiring support and understanding; uses active strategies for emotional regulation as language and the ability to represent ideas develop.

- Developing a sense of autonomy and a sense of initiative.

- Have increasing awareness of the needs of others, show more empathy for the feelings of others (as language develops, empathy becomes more reflective).

- Testosterone floods boys' brains and reduces their ability to control impulses, their behaviour is more irregular (adapted from Berk, 2006).

Human babies are born very immature and without the ability to regulate emotional reactions. Learning to take control of their emotions is a long drawn out process. The younger the child, the more they are at the mercy of their emotions so 'routine, familiarity and the presence of caring adults gives sanctuary to a child' (Robinson, 2009, p.180). Without being loved and valued, children cannot be expected to learn about care and respect for the feelings of others. In the Early Years it is the adults (caregivers, key persons) from whom children receive sensitive responses and Reception teachers who play significant roles in helping children learn to self-regulate. According to Shanker and Downer (2012) self-regulation is NOT self-control; it is the ability to manage environmental stresses to regain emotional balance and an optimum state of functioning. It is a 'child's ability to modulate her arousal states' (p.68). The ideal state of arousal is the *alert* state in which children are calm and they are able to concentrate. The *hypo and hyper-alert* states are on either side of the calm state. While hypo-alertness indicates loss of concentration and a drift into a drowsy, sleepy state, hyper-alert children get agitated and head towards the flooded state. The former requires up-regulation, the latter benefits from down-regulation. Physical activity can do both, for example, depending on the individual child. One child may need to run around to wake up and another may need it to calm down.

Some children need background music (an auditory stimulus) to keep them on task, to up-regulate from the hypo-alert state. Other children show signs of hyper-sensitivity to continuous noise, they start to fidget (sometimes even without realising that it is the noise level that puts this stress on them) and they lose concentration on the task at hand. Children's emotional thermostats respond to environmental stresses and move them along the continuum of arousal states. When in the hyper-alert state heading towards emotional flooding, children experience stress and they become agitated if not aggressive, they are highly impulsive, they cannot pay attention and they often crave sugary foods. The four main factors causing stress in children's lives are: lack of *sleep, noise/visual noise, stressed adults and food ('junk food' with high glycaemic index)* (Refer to Shanker, 2013 – Global Gathering conference talk). This has implications for how a learning environment is set up for children in a Reception class. Audio stimulus works for some children and disadvantages others. Colours on the walls, on the floor and colourful classroom equipment may be overwhelming for hyper-sensitive children while visual stimulus may work as an up-regulatory strategy for hypo-sensitive children. Because young children take their clues from the adults around them, over-tired teachers, fatigued or troubled parents may influence their arousal states in a negative way. Reception teachers who are able to self-regulate and who are attuned to the emotional needs of children in their class, can help children develop their own self-regulatory strategies. The teacher's consistent presence, the quality of relationship between the child and teacher and how the teacher views the child are key influencing factors in children's healthy emotional development. There is no master plan for emotional regulation; it is different and unique for every individual. There are four key steps, however, that a Reception teacher can follow to help children find what works for them (adapted from Shanker, 2010):

1. Be a detective: identify the stressor – it requires close observations.

2. Help children develop self-awareness – talk to children about their arousal states so they can understand what they are feeling and why.

3. Teach children what strategies work for them – monitor how children regulate themselves and help them with the trial and error process.

4. Share these strategies with the family so they can continue with supporting the child at home (develop a reciprocal relationship where teachers and parents learn from each other).

Point to ponder

How are noise levels monitored and controlled? Are you aware of the level of vibration and reverberation (how long it takes for the sound to disappear) in your classroom? Is it an echo-y room or have you got soft furnishings that absorb the noise?

(Continued)

(Continued)

Did you know: when children are stressed their middle ear function is cut out so they don't hear well?

Are you hypo- or hyper-sensitive to noise? Are you self-aware? Do you find teaching in a noisy environment exhausting or do you like the hustle and bustle? Do you have headphones for those children who need noise to up-regulate?

Have you got areas in your environment with neutral and pastel colours and areas that are more vibrant in colour? How can you create micro-environments with particular children in mind to help them learn self-regulation?

Adults' 'sensitive responsiveness' (Marrone, 1998, p.43) to these early experiences underpin healthy emotional development resulting in a seven year old having relatively strong optimal regulation which allows him to concentrate for a considerable length of time by ignoring distraction and controlling impulses reasonably well. Such a child is resilient, seeks help and is intrinsically motivated to learn. This brings me to another factor that influences emotional development: praise and external rewards.

The terms 'praise' and 'encouragement' are often used interchangeably or even combined to give meaning to one act. In terms of children's learning and emotional development the two terms are significantly different. Encouragement is often used by a Reception teacher as a strategy to motivate children to continue with their efforts. Praise, however, is a much contested term and concept and its effectiveness is questioned by Khon (1999) and Grille (2005). They feel that praising actually conditions children to seek approval of others and hinders the development of self-motivation. Both praise and external rewards (stickers, star charts, incentive plans, progression on a traffic light system, etc.) create addictive and dependent behaviour where children overlook the joy of achieving something, the feel good factor of getting something done for themselves. It takes away the intrinsic motivation from learning through curiosity, trial and error. The following key points, adapted from Khon (2000), explain why praise and rewards sometimes can be counter-productive with young children:

1. *They can manipulate children*: praising and rewarding children for complying with classroom rules, tidying away toys and play equipment, for example, can be seen as done for the teacher's convenience. It could be more effective to talk to children about how the group has benefited from a tidy classroom and how it makes them all feel.

2. *They can be addictive:* children can become dependent on the evaluation of the teacher, who gives the praise. More significantly, children can become reliant on the teacher's evaluation of what is good or bad rather than learn to make their own judgements on how well or badly they feel they have done something.

3. *They can steal the child's pleasure:* children should be able to feel proud of what they have accomplished and show their pleasure ('I have done it') without an adult dishing out the sticker or the verdict 'well done' immediately and with it stealing the child's joy.

4. *Praise and reward can lead to children losing interest:* by excessive praising and rewards children lose interest in what they get the praise for (e.g. painting, writing, modelling); instead, they become increasingly interested in getting the praise or the external rewards. The focus is not to do well in something (building a bridge between two buildings because they enjoy the activity, for example) but to win the teachers' praise and reward. In this way, engagement with the activity can be reduced to a surface level, it can become almost tokenistic and have one aim: to get rewarded.

5. *Praise and rewards can reduce achievement/progress:* when children become dependent on praise, they are less likely to take risks because they want to secure positive comments or rewards from the teacher. Risk taking is a pre-requisite for creativity, therefore critical thinking and progress.

6. *Praise and rewards administered publicly can be too much:* some children can find it very difficult to receive praise or reward publicly because of their insecure sense of self-worth or their emotional immaturity. Having to get up and to collect a certificate from the head teacher in front of the whole school may be excruciatingly painful and can become more of a stress than a reward.

This is not to say that Reception children should never be praised or rewarded. Rather, it is an invitation for Reception teachers to consider the timing, the frequency, the space and the content of the praise. Giving children time to self-evaluate first and being specific about what is appreciated or approved when praise is given help children become contented and self-assured. Children's self-worth is also strengthened by experiences such as overcoming difficulties, acknowledging own progress and coping with disappointment, so pointing these out to them could be more effective than praise. Intrinsic rewards have longer lasting effects than external ones.

Attunement, compassion, genuine interest from the teacher are what 'give momentum to daily acts of kindness' (Robinson, 2009, p.182) and lay the foundations for children's early emotional development and their emotional well-being. At school, it is the teachers who hold children's emotions for them while they are learning to manage and self-regulate themselves.

> **? Point to ponder**
>
> What effect do you think reward charts and stickers have on children? How do they compare with the teacher's genuine smile and approval? Do you tell other school adults and the parents in the child's presence when he/she gains your approval for an achievement? Have you got strategies to help children develop emotional self-awareness?

Conclusion

Learning is a deeply personal experience and this is particularly true for four year olds whose view of the world is rather egocentric. Because early childhood is a period of most rapid change, children in a Reception class are on a broad developmental spectrum. Each child's developmental curve and pace is unique to them and Reception teachers plan developmentally appropriate experiences that account for these individual characteristics, limitations and potentials, so progress is ensured. 'Teachers can "unlock" the gates but the [individual] pathways must have their own magic' (Gerver, 2011, p.107). Discovering this magic is what excites Reception teachers, this is what makes teaching this age group a most intensely satisfying profession, this is how teaching becomes a moral act (Paley, 1991). 'To teach is to touch a life forever' (Gerver, 2011, p.36).

Further inspiration

To hear Lilian Katz speaking about her thinking, visit https://www.youtube.com/watch?v=aiZW0jIngc8

References

Anderson, P. (2002) Assessment and development of executive function (EF) during childhood. *Child Neuropsychology*, 8: 71–82.

Argyle, M. (1994) *The psychology of interpersonal behaviour* (5th ed.). London: Penguin.

Bayley, N. (2005) *Bayley scales of infant and toddler development* (3rd ed.). San Antonio, TX: Harcourt Assessment.

Bercow, J. (2008) *The Bercow Report A review of services for children and young people with speech, language and communication needs*. Nottingham: DCSF Publications.

Berk, L.E. (2006) *Child development* (7th ed.). Boston, MA: Pearson International Edition.

Brown, S. (2008) Play is more than fun – TED talk https://www.youtube.com/watch?v=HHwXlcHcTHc

Bruce, T. and Meggitt, C. (2003) *Child care and education*. London: Hodder & Stoughton.

Bruner, J. (1983) *Child's talk: Learning to use language.* Oxford: Oxford University Press.

Cleave, S. and Brown, S. (1993) *Early to school. Four year olds in infant classes.* London: Routledge.

Corsaro, W. (2003) *We're friends, right?* Washington DC: Joseph Henry Press.

Diamond, A. (2002) Normal development of pre-frontal cortex from birth to young adulthood: Cognitive functions, anatomy and biochemistry, in D.T. Stuss and R.T. Knight (eds) *The frontal lobes.* London: Oxford University Press.

Doherty, J. and Hughes, M. (2014*) Child development theory and practice 0–11 (2nd ed.*). Harlow: Pearson.

Dowling, M. (2010) *Supporting young children's sustained shared thinking.* London: The British Association for Early Childhood Education.

Dunn, J. (2004) *Children's friendships: The beginnings of intimacy.* Oxford: Blackwell Publishing.

Edwards, C., Gandini, L. and Forman, G. (eds) (1998) *The hundred languages of children – The Reggio Emilia approach – Advanced reflections.* London: JAI Press Ltd.

Feeney, S., Moravcik, E. and Nolte, S. (2013) *Who am I in the lives of children? An introduction to early childhood education.* Boston, MA: Pearson Education.

Fisher, J. (2013) *Starting from the child.* Maidenhead: Open University Press.

Gallahue, D.L. and Ozmun, J.C. (1998) *Understanding motor development.* Boston, MA: McGraw Hill.

Gallahue D.L. and Ozmun, J.C. (2006) *Understanding motor development. Infants, children, adolescents, adults (*6th ed.). New York: McGraw Hill.

Gerver, R. (2011) *Creating tomorrow's schools today. Education – our children – their futures.* London: Continuum.

Goddard-Blythe, S. (2005) *The well-balanced child.* Stroud: Hawthorn Press.

Gopnik, A., Meltzoff, A. and Khul, P. (2001) *How babies think.* London: Phoenix.

Graddol, D., Chesire, J. and Swann, J. (1994) *Describing language (2nd ed.*). Maidenhead: Open University Press.

Grille, R. (2005) Rewards and praise: the poisoned carrot. 'You really worked hard on your picture!' Guiding with encouragement. *Young Children on the Web – Beyond the Journal. http://www.naturalchild.org/robin_grille/rewards_praise.html*

Hart, B. and Risley, T. (2003) The early catastrophe. The 30 million word gap by age 3. *American Educator,* Spring 2003. *Aft.org Accessed: http://isites.harvard.edu/fs/docs/icb.topic1317532.files/09-10/Hart-Risley-2003.pdf*

Hartup, W. (1989) Social relationships and their developmental significance. *American Psychologist,* 44 (2): 120–6.

Katz, L.G. (2011) Current perspectives on the early childhood curriculum, in R. House (ed.) (2011) *Too much too soon: Early learning and the erosion of childhood.* Stroud: Hawthorn Press.

Khon, A. (1999) *Punished by rewards: The trouble with gold stars, incentive plans, A's, praise and other bribes*. New York: Houghton Mifflin.

Laevers, F. (2006) Forward to basics! Deep-level-learning and the experiential approach. *Early Years: An International Research Journal*, 20 (2): 20–9, DOI: 10.1080/0957514000200203

Luff. P. and Kanyal, M. (2015) Maternal thinking and beyond: Towards a care-full pedagogy for early childhood. *Early Child Development and Care* 185 (11–12): 1748–62.

Marrone, M. (1998) *Attachment and interaction*. London: Jessica Kingsley.

Martens, R. (1978) *Joy and sadness in children's sports*. Champaign, IL: Human Kinetics.

Maude, P. (2001) *Physical children, active teaching: Investigating physical literacy*. Maidenhead: Open University Press.

National Literacy Trust (2005) *Why do so many children lack basic language skills?* A discussion paper. Talk to Your Baby Campaign, London: NLT.

Oates, J. Karmiloff-Smith, A. and Johnson. M.H. (2012) *Developing brains*. Maidenhead: Open University Press.

Parten, M.B. (1932) Social participation among pre-school children. *Journal of Abnormal and Social Psychology*, 27 (3): 243–69.

Paley, V.G. (1991) *The boy who would be a helicopter*. Cambridge, MA: Harvard University Press.

Penn, H. (2005) *Understanding early childhood*. Maidenhead: Open University Press.

Piaget, J. (1952) *The origins of intelligence in children*. New York: International University Press.

Rinaldi, C. (2005) Documentation and assessment: What is the relationship? in A. Clark, A.T. Kjorholt, and P. Moss (eds) (2005) *Beyond listening: Children's perspectives on early childhood services*. Bristol: Policy Press.

Robinson, M. (2009) *From birth to one: The year of opportunity*. Maidenhead: Open University Press.

Shanker, S. (2010) Self-regulation: calm, alert and learning. *Education Canada*, 50 (3): 4–7.

Shanker, S. and Downer, R. (2012) Enhancing the potential in children, in L. Miller and D. Hevey (2012) *Policy issues in the early years*. London: SAGE.

Thompson, P.M., Giedd, J.N., Woods, R.P., MacDonald, D., Evans, A.C. and Toga, A.W. (2000) Growth patterns in the developing brain detected by using continuum mechanical tensor maps. *Nature*, 404: 190–2.

Vygotsky, L. (1978) *Mind in society*. Cambridge, MA: Harvard University Press.

Wassenberg, R., Feron, F.J.M., Kessel, A.G.H., Hendriksen, J.G.M. and Jolles, J. (2005) Relation between cognitive and motor performance in 5- to 6-year-old children: Results from a large-scale cross sectional study. *Child Development*, 76: 1092–103. Available from: http://pub.maastrichtuniversity.nl/de8ef2e1-0ba0-4c41-8ba2-726f54142b50

Jottings

3 You as an advocate for Early Childhood

Samantha Weeks

In this chapter we will begin to consider:

- the role of the Reception teacher as an Early Childhood advocate;
- what it is that makes Early Childhood separate and ultimately connected to the wider field of education;
- how to remain connected and stay strong;
- education as democracy.

Introduction

Malaguzzi reassured us that children have a deep pocket where they hold their memories and experiences from their pre-school years. In a world of accountability that is increasingly based upon data and expectations for attainment, many schools have buckled under the pressure and have succumbed to the drive for data and some have bought in schemes to help them collect and manage data about children's attainment and progress. Whatever it is called this is all about standardising children and their outcomes. Within the world of Early Years we can still hold on to the remnants of professional judgement and knowledge being seen as the key form of assessing young children's learning.

Whilst discussing philosophy with Gandini, Malaguzzi explains:

Learning is the key factor on which a new way of teaching should be based, becoming a complementary resource to the child and offering multiple options, suggestive ideas and sources of support. Learning and teaching should not stand on opposite banks and just watch the river flow by; instead, they should embark together on a journey down the water. Through an active, reciprocal exchange, teaching can strengthen learning how to learn.

(Edwards et al., 1998, p.83)

How do we stay strong when we are only one person in our Early Years department? Or when regulatory authorities have asked for attainment data only? How do we remain strong and true to our beliefs if Year 1 colleagues feel that the children have 'just been playing and running free' all year in Reception, and that the real teaching of reading must now begin? Forgetting the significant number of children who are exceeding in their approach to expressive Arts, or who can pose tremendously curious and creative questions, are those same colleagues asking themselves how to make best use of those skills, adding extension and breadth?

This chapter will identify debates that have resonance for all educators, of which Reception teachers are an integral part. Often the world of Early Childhood Education and Care (ECEC) can find itself placed in its own unique bubble. This bubble is a place where we feel safe, and we use the language of Early Childhood, we understand learning through play and we understand the Characteristics of Effective Learning (DfE, 2012). We are also perhaps a little guilty of standing outside the perceived restrictions of delivering the National Curriculum here in England, or other curricula relevant to older children or in other national contexts. Perhaps part of our role as an advocate for Early Childhood is to see ourselves as one of the cogs that is turning the movement of education as a whole.

Let's now look at some ways to answer the fundamental challenges posed above.

Take strength from the children

Look at the children when they are deeply engaged in play. Take a moment to indulge in that observation (discussed in Chapter 7) when the children in your care are deeply involved in play that you have facilitated, developed, nurtured and supported as a result of the knowledge you have of their fascinations and motivations. The children are the only reason that teachers exist – remember that and feel proud.

Find others around you, locally or via social media

Being an advocate for Early Childhood is like being a member of a large, international club! Sergio Spaggiari, when he spoke about Loris Malaguzzi in 2003 at the International Conference in Reggio Emilia, explained that if childhood were a football team then Malaguzzi was the super fan. This analogy has such resonance of course in Italy, but the point is clear. We are connected in the sense that we believe in and truly understand the significance of Early Childhood.

Not many years ago we were lucky enough in England to be well supported by Local Authorities at a time where funding was plentiful. Many areas had advisory teams bursting with members of our childhood fan club, passionate, excited and motivated. The landscape has changed and many Local Authorities are no longer in this position. You may be a teacher in a lucky place and still have your friendly, knowledgeable advisor who organises 'cluster groups' for you, which focus on issues of Early Childhood that you want to discuss. However, many are not so lucky now – if so, it is time to organise your own! Social media is incredible for this and many of you will have found this out already. It is a way of being connected to those who are like-minded where ever we are in the world. If you are not a regular internet user or do not feel confident about digital devices, please do not be scared of Twitter, Pinterest and the old favourite, Facebook. These are all tremendous places to find the Early Childhood army that exists. By venturing into the digital world you will find wonderful, brave practitioners who share their practice so that you are filled up with ideas. There are groups of like-minded practitioners that have set up discussion groups so that hot topics can be discussed and, importantly, challenged.

Team talks and tasks

Put up a sheet of flip chart paper or a sheet of A3 paper inside one of your cupboards. Ask the team over the course of a week to note on it any topics they have heard in the media. The next week let everyone add any comments that they may have.

Remember your child development knowledge and expertise

The quality of children's experience in school may be affected by the pedagogical knowledge and qualifications of the staff working with them. In order to maintain rich, complex and stimulating environments where practitioners are more able to integrate playing and learning into practice (Pramling Samuelsson and Asplund Carlsson, 2008; Johansson and Pramling Samuelsson, 2009) there is evidence to suggest a correlation between adults' qualification and the quality of provision. The EPPE study has provided consistent evidence to support this notion and identifies among its findings over time that quality is strongly related to levels of qualification and professional development (Sylva et al., 2010). It is not a straightforward correlation and therefore the opposing conclusion cannot necessarily be drawn that children's experiences will be of poor quality when supported by adults without specific qualifications. However, the compelling evidence is related to the quality of interactions and understanding of play and there is evidence to demonstrate that specific early childhood professional development and training improves the quality of children's experiences (OECD, 2011).

> **? Point to ponder**
>
> When did you last relate your understanding of child development to your practice? Is there somebody that you can have that conversation with? Have you got a journal in which you could start to record your reflection on what you are seeing in your practice and why?

Blind with science

As mentioned in the introduction, educators in all fields are being asked increasingly to present data. Nobody wants this to distract from the time we spend with the children or preparing fabulous learning experiences for the children in our care. It is pertinent of course to ask about and ponder the relevance of this data, in terms of the experience that children are having on a day-to-day basis. The recent re-introduction of baseline assessments in England is an interesting example to consider. An intriguing situation therefore is the chain of events that have occurred after the collection of the first round of data for baseline. *Early Excellence* (a key provider of baseline assessment) is an outstanding organisation that embodies what many of us in the sector aspire to as excellent Early Years practice. Their response to the government's call for baseline data was to make it good: to turn what could be simply dreadful into an opportunity to underpin good practice. As a Reception teacher I attended one of their briefings and was so encouraged to hear that they were not going to focus on only Literacy and Mathematics, but on the characteristics of effective learning, wellbeing and involvement scales as well as all seven areas of learning. There was a general a sigh of relief, and a cry of 'halleluiah' from many Reception teachers. It could be argued that it is good practice to be making observations and judgements about children in all of these areas during their first half term in Reception, and for this reason the Early Excellence approach made sense to many – in fact 75 per cent – of the sector. At the time of writing, baseline assessment has been suspended.

Significantly now that the data is in, some of the analysis (not necessarily all of it) is providing evidence that could have an impact on practice that may surprise others, government included. Now that the Characteristics of Effective Learning are being 'measured' and reported on this is being included in the projection of children's future success. For example, a child who is demonstrating that they have an attitude to learning which means that they can 'have a go' and 'take risks' but happens to score below average in their Mathematics may well end up doing better by Year 6 than the child who scores high in Mathematics at the beginning of Reception but is not confident to 'take risks' with their learning. If we are clever (and we are), as an Early Years workforce we need to use this evidence to our benefit and most importantly to the benefit of children's education. Clearly this is becoming evidence to suggest that it is *how* children learn rather than *what* that could be a predictor of their future success! We know this – we need to be armed with the evidence to blind others with the science that proves it.

Remember that you are not alone!

Claxton and Lucas (2015, p.171) begin their concluding chapter *A Call for Action* with the following Piaget quote:

> *The principal goal of education in schools should be creating men and women who are capable of doing new things, not simply repeating what other generations have done; men and women who are creative, inventive and discoverers, who can be critical and verify, and not accept everything they are offered.*

The idea that schools should aim to foster the ability to be *creative, inventive*, a *discoverer* and encourage *critical* thinking resonates with much of what we strive to do in our interpretation and application of the EYFS in Reception classes in England and in good practice in Early Years education in other contexts. There is strength to be taken from this and encouragement to be taken from an increasingly vocal movement of academics (referred to as 'blobs' by policy makers in England not so long ago) who are arguing for a shift in the way that we organise education throughout. This is a moment at which those of us in an Early Childhood bubble need to look out and see the connections that bind us with the rest of the world of education. Claxton and Lucas identify 'confidence, curiosity, collaboration, communication, creativity, commitment and craftsmanship' as seven Cs that they argue should appear in every school curriculum (2015, p.74). These they describe as the habits of mind that will underpin lifelong learning. Once the public examinations have been passed and knowledge has been tested we must ask ourselves what it is that young people will need. Claxton and Lucas give the compelling example of teaching the Tudors in a way that 'develops the habits of independence, imagination, empathy and debate; or you can teach them in a way that develops passivity, compliance, credulity and memorisation' (2015, p.76). Their example suggests that the outcome initially could be the same, the test could well be passed. However, clearly the habits of learning that have been fostered are far more appealing and apparently useful for future life. Will Gompertz argues passionately for the ability to understand thinking and he explains his rationale for '*Thinking Like an Artist*' underpinning this powerful argument that if there 'ever was a time when we don't need to learn to regurgitate knowledge, it is now'. He urges that what the future generation will be able to do with that knowledge; that should be our concern (Gompertz, 2015).

Team talks and tasks

What does 'thinking like an artist' mean to you and your team? How can you demonstrate divergent and meaningful artistic approaches in your work and support children's thinking?

Figure 3.1 The boys have a clear idea about the clay man that they would like to build. Their ideas are their own, in response to a provocation and they have the time to follow their plan – and they are determined

Point to ponder

Which of Claxton's seven Cs can you identify here?

Democracy as an ideal and a habit

Dewey's words 'Education is not preparation for life: education is life' are well known. The connection between education and democracy as he saw it was visionary in his time and placed him as a progressive. His assertion that 'A democracy is more than a form of government; it is primarily a mode of associated living, of conjoint communicated experiences' (Dewey, 1916, p.10) is something that we find is deeply engrained in education rhetoric now. It is a poignant philosophy to consider though as we question what this tells us about the purpose of what we are aiming to achieve in our classrooms. Dewey explains:

> *When the immature human being becomes a co-partner ... in engaging in the conjoint activity, he has the same interest in its accomplishment, which others have. He shares ideas and emotions. In the cases when he really shares or participates in the common activity his original impulse is modified. He not merely acts in a way agreeing with the actions of others, but in so acting, the same ideas and emotions are aroused in him that animate the others.*

(Dewey,1916, pp.13–14)

Considering these wise words can remind us that there is a democratic purpose behind our work with young children and it is important. This is surely an aspect of our work that we should be advocates for.

Figure 3.2 Making decisions together, forming the foundations of democracy

Democracy in everyday practice: It's all about the rainbows!

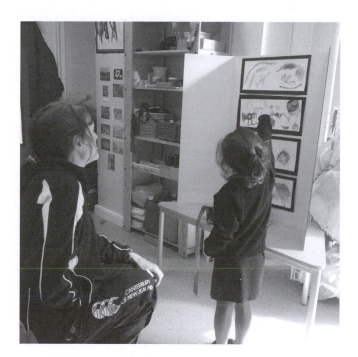

Figure 3.3 Explaining what the exhibition is about

The children had produced a huge range of artwork that had evolved from our project looking at 'rainbows'. Together after much discussion we decided to put on an exhibition. The children made the invitations and decided who they would like to invite. They worked with Christine (wonderful teaching assistant) to create a menu of snacks for our visitors and they decided on the jobs that each would have. The photograph demonstrates one of our 'guides' explaining to her PE teacher what our exhibition is all about. The children made the decisions in partnership with us, and shared the responsibility for fulfilling the plans that we had made jointly.

Further binding the world of Early Childhood to the rest of the world of education is this notion of democracy. Peter Moss has written extensively about the Early Childhood institution as a place of democracy (Moss, 2008). Democracy is rooted in many of the ideals of Reggio Emilia; the place Howard Gardner said he could see social constructivism happening in front of his eyes (Giudici et al., 2001). Vygotsky taught us that learning is essentially social in nature, the idea that we learn from each other through a complex mesh of reciprocal relationships can be allowed to form the bedrock of democracy. Moss reminds us that:

> *Any vision of education that takes democracy seriously cannot but be at odds with educational reforms which espouse the language and values of market forces and treat education as a commodity to be purchased and consumed.*
>
> (Carr and Hartnett, 1996 cited in Moss, 2011, p.1)

The language of market forces is alive and well, it sits comfortably within debates surrounding 'league tables', 'predictors', 'progress indicators' – the list is recognisable and goes on. In order to maintain practice that is built on the fundamentals of democracy, as practitioners we need to be:

> *more attentive to creating possibilities than pursuing predefined goals… {to be} removed from the fallacy of certainties, {assuming instead} responsibility to choose, experiment, discuss, reflect and change, focusing on the organisation of opportunities rather than the anxiety of pursuing outcomes, and maintaining in {our} work the pleasure of amazement and wonder.*
>
> (Fortunati 2006, p.37)

Fortunati reminds us that it is our responsibility to make this happen. While we are bound by policies and government initiatives, in the classroom it is us. We have the skills and abilities to *choose, experiment, discuss, reflect* and *change*.

Conclusion

It is my hope in closing this chapter that it can support you in finding strength and a sense of belonging in the Early Childhood place in which you find yourself. We are connected by our membership of this fan club called childhood and we, together, have the responsibility of ensuring that it is the best that we can make it.

 Point to ponder

Do I remind myself regularly to look at the children and appreciate the quality of the play that they are engaged in, facilitated by me?

Can I use social media to share ideas, build my confidence and find others that understand?

(Continued)

(Continued)

Is there a course locally or virtually that I can enrol on to build my library of science that I can 'blind' others with? Use the OECD evidence above to explain your rationale for this to your head teacher, Board of Governors or line management.

Figure 3.4 Knowing the children in your care and matching the provision to their needs and interests

Further inspiration

Some useful organisations and web-based opportunities to join the debate:

Save Childhood Movement http://www.savechildhood.net

Early Years Foundation Stage Forum http://eyfs.info/home

EYTalking@EYTalking

#eytstwitterpals

Children and nature network http://www.childrenandnature.org

References

Carr, W. and Hartnett, A. (1996) *Education and the struggle for democracy*. Maidenhead: Open University Press.

Claxton, G. and Lucas, B. (2015) *Educating Ruby: What our children really need to learn*. Ceredigion: Crown.

Department for Education (2012) *Statutory Framework for the Early Years Foundation Stage*. Runcorn: Department for Education.

Dewey, J. (1916) *Democracy and education: An introduction to the philosophy of education*. New York: Macmillan.

Edwards, C., Gandini, L. and Forman, G. (Eds) (1998) *The hundred languages of children: The Reggio Emilia approach – advanced reflections (2nd ed.)*. Greenwhich, CT: Ablex Publishing.

Fortunati, A. (2006) *The Education of Young Children as a Community Project*. Azzano San Paulo, Brazil: Edizioni Junior: 34–37.

Giudici, C., Rinaldi, C. and Krechevsky, M. (Eds) (2001) *Making learning visible: Children as individual and group learners*. Cambridge, MA: Project Zero; Reggio Emilia, Italy: Reggio Children.

Gompertz, W. (2015) *Think Like An Artist* (Public lecture at Stamford Endowed Schools) 27 November 2015.

Johansson, E. and Pramling Samuelsson, I. (2009) To weave together: Play and learning in early childhood education. *Journal of Australian Research in Early Childhood Education*, 16 (1): 33–48.

Moss, P. (2008) What future for the relationship between early childhood education and care and compulsory schooling? *Research in Comparative and International Education,* 3 (3): 1.

OECD (2011) *Research brief: Encouraging Quality in Early Childhood Education and Care.* Paris: OECD.

Pramling Samuelsson, I. and Asplund Carlsson, M. (2008) The playing learning child: Towards a pedagogy of early childhood. *Scandinavian Journal of Educational Research*, 52 (6): 623–41.

Sylva, K., Melhuish, E., Sammons, P., Siraj-Blatchford, I. and Taggart, B. (2010) *Early childhood natters: Evidence from the Effective Pre-school and Primary Education project*. London/New York: Routledge.

Jottings

4 You as a collaborator in learning

Claire Underwood, Anna Cox and Gillian Sykes

In this chapter we will begin to consider:

- what it looks like to be a collaborator in learning with children;
- what it means to be a learning partner and the value of co-constructing new learning;
- what this might look like in practice;
- examples from Claire's and Gillian's practice to challenge and stimulate your thinking.

Introduction

This chapter is in many ways less organised than the other chapters are, partly as a result of our divergent thinking and partly because as a collaborator you are not in charge. This will be illustrated by the examples from Claire's and Gillian's practice, which will say more than theory can much of the time, as indeed should our thinking about those examples which we have tried to share honestly.

The Early Years setting is bursting at the seams with stories. Thinking of all the 'threads' of play of individuals, pairs, groups or the entire community can be overwhelming. Every adult in the setting seeks to develop and extend these threads sensitively and it is a skill to be mastered. Common terms to describe adult actions during play are modelling and scaffolding.

Wood et al. (1976, p.90) describe scaffolding as an 'adult controlling those elements of the task that are essentially beyond the learner's capacity, thus permitting him to concentrate upon and complete only those elements that are within his range of competence'. What does that mean for a Reception teacher? It means knowing each child well enough to gently push the boundaries of their learning. How can we ensure that when we join children in play we are not 'hijacking' it? How can we support the child without twisting the play to suit an adult agenda and in doing so reduce its meaning and motivation for the children? It's a tricky dance and we know that our clumsy feet have knotted up the 'threads of play' many a time. It is so tempting to turn an imaginative play story in the home corner into a counting opportunity but with too many misplaced questions the child is soon not going to feel like 'mum cooking dinner' and be simply a student answering questions to fulfil the needs of the teacher. That is not what they want and it should not be what we want.

To scaffold or not to scaffold

Vignette

Imagine a scene from a Reception class we know – a group of children within the setting who play together consistently choosing imaginative play. Able to observe from the outside but wanting to participate within their play their teacher (Claire!) crawled under the table 'den' that they had created and began to find out more about their play. They patiently explained the various roles of their play, she understood that it was to do with a television programme called Monster High *but she could not grasp the narrative of what was happening. Her suggestions felt out of place as they delicately negotiated their imagined situations. Throughout the time of teaching them she planned opportunities which followed this interest of* Monster High *with writing opportunities to do with the characters and adding enhancements to the block area which extended their play. However, she never managed to be involved in their imaginative play and did she really need to be? She thinks not.*

In this example much was learnt about the children and directions for future provision gathered but scaffolding was not right in that situation. This could be for a number of reasons and one of the most interesting is the relationship of the children's knowledge of the focus of their play. It is likely that they share the common interest in *Monster High* but had different knowledge and experience of it. We speculate that this would allow some magic to happen between them, that they were working in what is known as the 'zone of proximal development' or ZPD. This concept was explained by the well-respected Russian psychologist Lev Vygotsky (1896–1934). Interestingly scaffolding is not a term that Vygotsky used (Stone, 1998), but he did emphasise the role of social interaction as crucial to cognitive development and coined the term ZPD. This is when a child (in this case, though it could be an adult) learns with a more capable peer, working at a 'distance between the child's actual developmental level as determined by independent problem solving and the higher level of potential development as determined through problem solving under adult guidance and in collaboration with more capable peers' (Vygotksy, 1978, p. 86). What this boils down to is another who knows a bit more being able to help to bridge the gap between what could be learnt alone and what can be learnt with enabling help. The *Monster High* fans are very likely to have been doing this kind of learning together.

Relationship building to support teacher–child collaboration

The numerous relationships between a Reception teacher and the children in the class are intimate. But relationships take time to build. Some children will straightaway be happy to invite you into their play and to respond to your suggestions and to develop play collaboratively. However, other relationships take a lot longer to build. The challenges of building and sustaining relationships in the Reception class are numerous and they are very different to other situations. Negotiating meaningful relationships means that teachers have to be open and emotionally authentic. This is a theme in other parts of this book too. For the purposes of this chapter the following words explain it well:

The more real I am to my students, the more open they are to me. When I nurture this kind of relationship it carries over into the kind of learning that blossoms into life-changing moments and revolutionary thinking.

(Stinson, as cited in Nieto, 2005, p.109)

Vignette

This is another example from Claire's practice:

The child we are thinking about had arrived in the country a fortnight before beginning school. He had no English apart from being taught her name 'Mrs Underwood' by his older siblings in anticipation of the home visit. During the time spent with him in his home he was deeply engaged with playing on a tablet, only giving me small glances as his interests and motivations were discussed. How would he cope starting school after already having a huge upheaval in his life? As ever the resilience of children surprised me as he found himself in a community of lots of children and begun to settle into a brand new environment. Adults in the classroom had set out the small world with cars and vehicles in response to listening to lots of the new children having a love for this in their home visits and through observations during the stay and plays. Our focus child quickly found a 'Lightning McQueen' car which captured his interest and distracted him briefly from being away from his home and family. Luckily I had some very patient teachers in Year 6 who had taught me some basic Somali phrases such as 'Mummy will be back soon' and 'Do you need the toilet?' She had these written phonetically on an iPad and the spark of surprise in the child's eyes when he heard them from this new adult helped him begin to settle and feel included. He soon got to know the rhythms and routines of the day and it wasn't long before there were no longer tears and his mother told me that he looked forward to coming and even asked to come to school when it was the weekend! He had strong interests in his play choosing the cars, dinosaurs or riding the bikes outside. We had brief moments of playing together with the tap-a-shapes and building a train track in the block play. There was no 'pressure' to 'play' with Claire, and I often played alongside him contentedly verbalising a running commentary of what I was doing and the thought processes behind it.

Trust

This gentle model of relationship building does not deny the fact that as teachers we have to have some degree of premeditation in our interactions with children, but our plans and intentions must be fluid. Otherwise we become dictators not collaborators. We suggest that empathy is a secure starting point for collaboration but is not enough on its own. The key feature of being effective in working in collaboration with children is trust. In an American school study researchers Bryk and Schneider (2004) identified three kinds of trust, which they call organic trust, contractual trust and relational trust. Organic trust is the kind with individuals that is based on implicit faith and a good example of this is the trust people might have in their religious beliefs and is not appropriate in our relationships with children. Contractual trust is the trust individuals have within some kind of prescribed relationship – you want to know the person fitting your new bathroom will fit the bath you want and it won't leak. This kind of trust really does often reside in contracts and again is not relevant to our relationships with children in our classes. The kind of trust we are interested in is relational trust. Bryk and Schneider use the term for trust in communities where individuals know their own role and that of others, they know the interaction between these roles and have confidence they will be lived up to. We think this is the kind of trust that will exist in your classroom and which will enable you to be a collaborator in learning. Children do not for one minute mistake you for another child but they come to understand the teacher you are and that you have their best interest at heart, that you care about them and that you can indeed be trusted.

There are also biological elements to trust and one of these is the hormone oxytocin. This is what is sometimes called the bonding chemical, it is most often talked about in the context of birth. Wade (2006) found that oxytocin substantially increases levels of trust. This goes some way to explain the sense of being bonded to children that we teach and their fond attachments to us when trust has been built between us.

Slow time

How does the Reception teacher behave during periods of immersive and collaborative play? In her practice Claire and her team use the 'Adult pedagogic strategies self-evaluation framework' from the Pen Green Research Centre (Whalley et al., 2005; Pen Green, 2007) to reflect upon and develop practice.

Vignette

Here is Claire's description of a rainy day at her setting, still thinking about the same focus child.

Adults and children are outside whatever the weather and there is a class set of waterproof all-in-one suits and wellington boots to enable this to happen. For some children to put on this strange suit and boots is a risk and many are not too keen to do so when they join the setting. However, on this rainy

(Continued)

(Continued)

day she noticed the child watching the other children, who were having a mucky messy time in the mud kitchen, with interest. She asked him, accompanied with signing, if he would like to put on a suit and join them. He shook his head. When they turned on the outside tap and the children began transporting the water to create a huge muddy puddle Claire noticed him watching again. She asked him again if he wanted to join in and put a suit on. He nodded and she followed him around to where children get changed into the suits and supported him to put on a suit. He looked up at her and she nodded and smiled and indicated that they might go and join in. Once in the mud kitchen she began modelling making a mixture and mixing it up in one of the saucepans, modelling the language that he would need. Once he was set up with a spoon and a mixture she moved away a little and dug up spoonfuls of mud and offered them to him to put in his mixture saying 'more?'. He repeated the word so they kept playing this for a little while. He looked around and found himself a small pot and walked off towards the running tap with a purposeful stride. He shrieked with excitement when he saw the massive muddy puddle and as he gingerly jumped over it he looked at another child with the look that just said 'Can you believe we are really doing this?' He engaged in play around the puddle filling up the pot and transporting it back to his mixture in the mud kitchen. As time went on he took more risks and explored more of his own ideas. Selecting a large watering can and filling it up with the muddy water, he then began creating another puddle in the hole that had been dug out by another child up near the mud kitchen. During the play he was involving Claire, handing out resources for her to use and responding to her suggestions through gesture and some repeated words. She described having felt overwhelmed with the privilege of being able to show a child the wonder and enjoyment of playing in this open-ended, natural way. 'You can feel the frisson of learning when you are engaged with a child in this kind of play' she said.

Figure 4.1 A child enjoying his kind of play

Reception teachers need to be confident to spend their time in the mud with members of their class. The view from another classroom or over the school fence can see this sharing of slow time with children as trivial. We use the expression slow time here to indicate the times when you are supporting a child and collaborating with them at a pace dictated by them, as trust develops. It takes courage to let go of any sense of control over what is happening when others are looking over your shoulder. Be brave, you are the expert and can justify your pedagogy.

Point to ponder

Do you feel confident to see 'slow time' as important to your practice? Can you see how the saying 'more is less' fits with this approach?

Emotional contagion

The expression emotional contagion (Powell and Kusuma-Powell, 2010) is a useful one in describing collaboration in learning. It happens when two or more people are relating well and it is how emotions are shared. For this to happen, there must not be a power relationship between the parties, and this is illustrated well in our next example from Claire's practice. Here she describes collaboration in learning and emotional contagion takes place again with the very same child!

Vignette

Claire describes what happens when it was time to get cleared up and tidied away.

The boy's boots made a funny 'sucking' sound as I helped him to pull them off his sodden feet. He and I exclaimed and laughed together at the water pouring out and at his saturated socks and remarked at the 'cosy' feeling of putting warm socks on after his feet were dried.

Positive emotions as she collaborated with this child enabled him to be confident about something that might have been a source of anxiety. When his mother came to collect him they looked at the photographs that had been taken together. He was talking animatedly about this experience and mum was translating for me. When the doors were opened the following day the child went straight to the suits and called over to her with eyes full of anticipation of more muddy play. Experiences like this enjoyed together build relationships.

In the moment

To be 'present' with a child for a sustained amount of time can be tricky in a whole group of children and adults who all have their own ideas and agendas. It takes the instinct of the teacher to know which thread of play and learning to follow and for how long. There are many times when a child has been supported to get their suits and boots on, begun play in the mud kitchen, and then after a moment when the teacher turns to another child, then they have moved away and begun another line of play.

The 'conker' vignette in Chapter 5 describes a successful time of sustained shared thinking when Claire had felt genuinely curious and empowered the child to lead the thinking. 'Why had the conker split?' Researching together they developed a joint understanding, which Caleb then put to good use. However, choosing when to dedicate this time and energy into one 'thread' of play can be tricky. As discussed earlier this is often instinctive but at other times the children tell you in other ways. Sharing your energies and time with another of the 30 children in your care can often mean that our attention is diverted. This conker example demonstrates how a thread of play and sustained shared thinking can occur with the teacher moving in and out of it at certain times. But this is only successful if the adult has empathy and an authentic interest in the children's lines of inquiry. Fortunately, for Claire, Caleb's earnest persistence resulted in her seeing the depth of his understanding.

Point to ponder

How do you share your time between the 30 diverse characters in your class? Or do you? How can you make sure that all children feel included and valued?

Building learning with your 'trusty team'

The 'trusty team' referred to here consists of everyone in your class, children and adults. It surprises us that teachers ever feel the need to plan in isolation. Involving children in planning their learning is a simple yet powerful tool to capture and maintain their engagement. Claire refers to this in Chapter 5 when she talks about planning around the story of the 'Gingerbread Man'. Initially children may feel hesitant and unsure, but by showing your interest and valuing their ideas they quickly understand that their views are listened to and respected. Malaguzzi (2000) would refer to this as the 'pedagogy of listening', so eloquently described in the 'The Hundred Languages of Children'. Very quickly an ethos of planning as a trusty team is developed. Adults respond and generate learning opportunities based on the children's suggestions. However, we have got to have faith in this planning technique and be able to put your trust in your children. Children, just like adults, love to bounce ideas off each other. One idea will lead to another, and then to another and so it goes on.

Vignette

Here Gillian describes her experience at the end of a long term.

She asked the children what they might like to learn about next term. A list emerged including Shrek, New York, fairies, mermen and racing cars. When the children returned after their break the ideas were revisited and during a 'project meeting' (adults and children) the children were asked which they would like to learn about first. Shrek was their democratic choice and Gillian and her team set to work planning with them, what they wanted to do, and generating ideas for the continuous provision and enhanced provision. Her trusty team began to involve their families and resources and other ideas came flooding in. Shrek was just a vehicle for the children to learn through and to enable them to express themselves in their own way. 'We became true to children's ideas'.

It is clear in this example that children were regarded as active social agents (Kinney and Wharton, 2015). Planning and reviewing their learning, and engaging in meaningful exchanges to develop and extend their ideas were valued by Gillian and the other adults she worked with. By reviewing the learning, the children were able to reflect on their experiences, and engage in metacognition. Children were quickly able to use the language of learning.

Team talks and tasks

How might you engage in 'project planning' with your children? How might you use the 'Hundred Languages of Children' to enhance your provision?

The diversity of interests

If we then trust children to plan effectively, we can also trust them to be inspired by their peers. Gillian describes herself as often inspired by something she has read, or something someone has said or done. Children are much the same. One child might come to school with an interest in Thomas the Tank Engine, but in a few days this interest has changed to Spiderman. Being a superhero with your friends is far more appealing than playing by yourself with a train. In the same way, exciting projects can evolve through one child's interest.

Vignette

In a class that Gillian taught Shannon was a quiet little girl who found it difficult to engage with other children and found it difficult to spend time away from her mummy. Her interests were simple: her family (mum, dad, brother), Skegness (her favourite place in the world) and Harry and the Bucketful of Dinosaurs (her favourite book). In an effort to help her engage in learning Gillian asked if she would like to bring in her favourite book. Bingo! This lit the spark which then ignited a flame. Shannon stood before the class and 'read' her book to them. She then led the children in planning their learning resulting from this starting point. What started as one moment, ended up as six weeks of dinosaurs present in every imaginable way. Gillian and her trusty team had come to a 'crisis' point with Shannon. By reflecting with each other (adults) and then with Shannon, in a culture of openness and trust they were able to transform learning. Not just for Shannon, but for the children and adults in the class.

This is a super example to demonstrate the saying 'from tiny acorns mighty oak trees grow', or as Malaguzzi would say 'when it is the children (who) give shape to things'. 'Taking action takes courage. Taking action as a result of listening to children means sometimes having to change decisions already made' (Kinney and Wharton, 2015, p.2).

Figure 4.2 An example of planning through children's ideas and questions

Point to ponder

How might you document your planning with children? How might you also involve parents and families in this planning process?

Children as theorists

Anna, in Chapter 9, examines the role of the children and adults being researchers, and the idea of the children and adults forming a learning community. As we are looking here at the children and adults being collaborators in learning we would like to investigate the concept of the children and adults as theorists, working together to develop theories, make connections and to construct hypotheses. Many of the chapters in this book can be referred to here. For example, we need to observe children to know when and how we can intervene, we need to provide environments and experiences which enable children to speculate and contemplate. Malaguzzi (2012) would describe this as children being involved as meaning makers. Making sense of their world. 'Learning is focused on the process of the children's explorations, not the end product' (Hay, in Bancroft et al., 2008, p.3). Children engaged in this type of learning will exhibit high levels of well-being and involvement. Together the adult and child record, then document this episode of learning. Together they make sense of what has happened and provide documentation for others to learn from their theories, and to make learning visible to others. These might be in the form of a learning story (see Chapter 9) or a documentation poster. Whatever form the documentation takes it needs to be:

- professional, as this puts value on the children's work;

- a combination of the children's and adults' voices, celebrating collaborative working;

- aesthetically pleasing, so that people will want to read it;

- multi modal – e.g. photographs, children's pictures, writing, different fonts;

- shared with a range of audiences to encourage discussion.

Documentation invites enquiry about children's thinking ... Documentation is a research report used to enhance discourse rather than a record of a past event.

(Edwards et al., 2012, p.254)

Team talks and tasks

If pedagogical documentation is something new to your team then have a go at writing a learning story or creating a documentation poster. Use the quotation above to support your work.

Conclusion

The notion of a collaborator conjures up a host of different roles – a double agent, or a spy. In some ways we are just that, as we work with the child to find out more about them. They are letting us into their world to enable us to tune into their interests and to interact meaningfully. A collaborator is also viewed as a co-worker or a team mate. We like this analogy as the shift of power is more balanced with the child and adult working together to construct learning as partners. We are given the privileged position of being able to witness their talents, gifts, feelings and perspectives. We can begin to learn about their views and opinions, and are given a ticket in to the most wonderful world of children.

Further inspiration

You must have a look at the lovely book by Robin Duckett and Mary Jane Drummond called *Adventuring in early childhood education*. The title is itself exciting and looks at how projects, inspired by children, and followed by adults, grow and develop.

Engage in explorations with your children taking ideas from Keri Smith's book, *How to be an explorer of the world: Portable life museum*.

Read *The girl with the brown crayon* by Vivian Gussin Paley and learn how, by following the children's interests, and being a teacher willing to be taught by your students, great things will unfold.

Download and display 'The Hundred Languages of Children' and look for the hundred, hundred more languages in your classrooms.

Explore some of the projects on the website of 5x5x5 http://5x5x5creativity.org.uk

This interesting piece from Australia uses the term 'intentional' in describing the roles of both adults and children. Read it and think about your own intentions when you collaborate in children's learning.

http://www.earlychildhoodaustralia.org.au/our-publications/australasian-journal-early-childhood/index-abstracts/ajec-vol-38-4-2013/1850-2/

References

Bancroft, S., Fawcett, M. and Hay, P. (Eds) (2008) *Researching children researching the world: 5x5x5=creativity.* Stoke-on-Trent: Trentham Books.

Bryk, A. and Schneider, B. (2004) *Trust in schools: A core resource for development.* New York: Russell Sage.

Edwards, C., Gandini, L. and Forman, G. (Eds) (2012) *The hundred languages of children (3rd* ed.). California: Praeger.

Kinney, L. and Wharton, P. (2015) *An encounter with Reggio Emilia: Children and adults in transformation (2nd ed.).* London: Routledge.

Malaguzzi, L., in Edwards, C., Gandini, L. and Forman, G. (Eds) (2012) *The hundred languages of children (3rd* ed.). California: Praeger.

Nieto, S. (Ed.) (2005) *Why we teach.* New York: Teachers College Press.

Pen Green (2005) Adult Pedagogic Strategies. Unpublished paper.

Powell, W. and Kusuma-Powell, O. (2010) *Becoming an emotionally intelligent teacher.* Thousands Oaks, CA: Corwin.

Stone, A. (1998) The metaphor of scaffolding: Its utility for the field of learning disabilities. *Journal of Learning Disabilities*, 3 (4): 344–64.

Vygotsky, L. (1978) *Mind in society: The development of higher psychological processes.* M. Cole, V. John-Steiner, S. Scribner and E. Souberman (Eds). Cambridge, MA: Harvard University Press.

Wade, N. (2006) *Before the dawn: recovering the lost history of our ancestors.* New York: Penguin Books.

Whalley, M. and the Pen Green Centre Team (2007) *Involving parents in their children's learning (2nd ed.).* London: Paul Chapman Publishing/Sage.

Wood, D.J., Bruner, J.S. and Ross, G. (1976). The role of tutoring in problem solving. *Journal of Child Psychiatry and Psychology*, 17(2): 89–100.

Jottings

5 You as creator of the learning environment

Samantha Weeks and Claire Underwood

In this chapter we will begin to consider:

- the relationship between pedagogy, knowledge of child development and the organisation of the learning environment;
- the significance of developing a shared understanding among your team in order to create an effective enabling environment;
- the unique nature of our individual classrooms;
- the role that children can have in creating their learning environments and opportunities.

Figure 5.1 Collaborative artwork inspired by Kandinsky and Rainbows

Introduction

The introduction of the EYFS (DfES, 2012) in England as a play-based, child-centred and principle-led framework meant many things to many people. For the purposes of this chapter the principle of 'Enabling Environments' is a helpful starting point and should have resonance with other relevant Early Childhood frameworks. The principle outlines that 'children learn and develop well in enabling environments, in which their experiences respond to their individual needs and there is a strong partnership between practitioners and/or carers'. We are reminded that the environment consists of the emotional and the physical as well as the indoor and the outdoor environment. Here we will concentrate on the indoor environment, as the outdoor environment will be considered in Chapter 6. Of course, this principle of 'Enabling Environments', although so relevant here, should not be seen alone and we must discuss it in relation to the other three principles:

- A Unique Child: 'Every child is a unique child, who is constantly learning and can be resilient, capable, confident and self-assured'

- Positive Relationships: 'Children learn to be strong and independent through positive relationships'

- Learning and Development: 'Children develop and learn in different ways and at different rates.'

The EYFS reminds us at the bottom of every page of the development matters document. This is also clear within the Learning and Development principles and many of us are happy with that. In Chapter 2 Eleonora quotes Malaguzzi and his analogy of 'spaghetti' to describe the unique journey that children may make through this journey of early development. If we believe that, then this must have implications for our expectations of children. As Thornton and Brunton identify, if this is a guiding principle then we probably expect children to 'have their own ideas, express their own opinions, make independent choices and play and work well with others' (2007, p.11). In order to facilitate this, children will need an environment that is filled with adults who believe this and want to nurture these characteristics. Malaguzzi (Edwards et al., 1998, p.62) described school for young children 'as an integral, living organism, as a place of shared lives and relationships among many adults and very many children'. 'We think of a school as a construction in motion, continuously adjusting itself' (Edwards et al., 1998, p.63). This would suggest that a school should be a place of discovery and exploration, a place where a significance is placed upon the building of relationships; underpinned by an understanding that this will be forever evolving. This chapter will explore these notions and unpick the emphasis we have in the Early Years, and must have in Reception classes, on the learning environment. It is more than a place to put 'stuff' and decorate, it is an integral part of the children's learning which directly reflects who we think that they are.

Shared understanding

A Reggio pre-school is a special kind of place, one in which young human beings are invited to grow in mind, in sensibility and in belonging to a broader community.

(Bruner, 1997, p.46)

Gandini (Edwards et al., 1989) clearly emphasises the significance of the 'environment' in children's experience and identifies that within the Reggio Emilia philosophy it is commonly referred to as the 'third teacher', the first and second being other children and adults. At the heart of everything in Reggio Emilia is a prized image of a child. It is this that drives all practice and all pedagogy:

Our image of children no longer considers them as isolated and egocentric, does not only see them as engaged in action with objects, does not emphasise only the cognitive aspects, does not belittle feelings or what is not logical and does not consider with ambiguity the role of the reflective domain. Instead our image of the child is rich in potential, strong, powerful, competent and, most of all, connected to adults and children.

(Malaguzzi in Penn, 1997, p.117)

This deeply held philosophical approach is the basis therefore of the design of the learning environments, the role of the adults within each school and the basis of debate that drives the *progettizione* (projects). In order to illustrate this further it is helpful to look at the characteristics identified by Malaguzzi in turn and consider the application in practice.

Rich in potential: This would be evident in interactions between adults and children, children and children, children and their environment. Significantly the evidence for this, it could be argued, is seen in the documentation that such emphasis is placed upon in Reggio Emilia. Observing children, documenting this and using the documentation itself as a way of moving learning forward places value on what it is that the child is saying, doing and wanting to learn. The display of documentation in this way is an integral part of the learning environments in Reggio Emilia and clearly demonstrates the image of a child.

Strong, powerful: Interesting to consider whether we agree that all children are indeed strong and powerful. There is clearly scope for discussion here and perhaps a point to ponder is whether we believe that children have the potential to be strong and powerful. If this is true then perhaps also we believe that children should be included in significant decisions in accordance with the UNCRC Article 12. Included in a way that is honest and meaningful, that fosters an understanding and belief in democracy. Decision making and sharing is part of the day in Reggio Emilia; each day starts with debate and discussion. Again, the learning environment reflects this physically and emotionally.

Competent: This would be evident in the way in which adults trust children. If they are seen as competent then they are capable, descriptions that suggest adults have high expectations of what children can already do. This is further evidence of the notion that children are citizens of now; rather than learning how to be an 'adult' they are a person in their own right. This particular construct of childhood encourages a view that is not overtly patronising; it is rather built on the idea of mutual respect. Therefore *competent* children would need an environment that was worthy of them, one which was not overly simplified and made specifically different to an adult working space. If we as adults enjoy working in aesthetically pleasing, calm, ordered, inspiring spaces then surely *competent* children would too.

Connected to adults and children: Evident in relationships inside, outside and with the environment. As Malaguzzi identifies, rather than seeing children as 'isolated and egocentric' his image is one that sees children as full members of their community. This is an intriguing concept that encourages debate in terms of how much we focus on the ways that children work as part of a group as opposed to individuals. Pertinent is the way in which we assess children; is it always as an individual or as a member of a group?

 Point to ponder

Rich in potential: Is there evidence in your classroom that you believe that children are rich in potential?

Strong and powerful: Pick a day, and honestly ask yourself how many meaningful decisions children were involved in about events that affected them directly?

Competent: Do the competent children in your classroom have an environment which is worthy of them – uncluttered, ordered and cared for? Sometimes the answer to this question is tricky as, honestly, we have different personal responses to the aesthetics of our environment. Think about the diversity of living rooms we have among us.

Connected to adults and other children: How explicit is your environment in valuing children as a member of a community?

So, we can see that the design of our learning environment is more than the placing of our resources, indeed the placing of those resources should be reflecting our carefully considered and constructed vision of childhood.

Figure 5.2 Children who have the time and space to demonstrate that they are rich in potential, strong and powerful as well as competent and connected to each other

Putting principles into practice

Elizabeth Jarman's work on developing *Communication Friendly Spaces©* is a recent example of an approach to re-designing and looking at our learning environments in a way that encourages engagement rather than overstimulation and is rooted in pedagogical discussion. Pertinent to further consideration is a recent study from Salford University, *Clever Classrooms* (Barrett et al., 2015). This study identifies clear evidence of the effect of classroom design on children's learning. They discuss three types of physical characteristics of the classroom: stimulation (appropriate level of complexity and colour), individualisation (ownership and flexibility) and naturalness (light, temperature and air quality). They explain that:

> *Surprisingly, whole-school factors (e.g. size, navigation routes, specialist facilities, play facilities) do not seem to be anywhere near as important as the design of the individual classrooms. This point is*

reinforced by clear evidence that it is quite typical to have a mix of more and less effective classrooms in the same school. The message is that, first and foremost, each classroom has to be well designed.

(Barrett et al., 2015, p.3)

The study finds that very small inexpensive changes can make substantial differences; for example, changing the layout of the room, the choices of display or colour of the walls. This brings us back to the notion that it is important to look closely at the environment that you have and how it can best support the children you work with and be understood by the team you are part of. This is not a scenario where we can rely on what has been in a classroom previously. An example that perhaps many of us relate to is that of primary-coloured ceiling hanging displays, the purpose of which many well-intentioned Reception teachers would have argued would have been to 'jolly' up the classroom, to make it feel like a child's place. By considering this, though, at a deeper level and looking at the type of evidence that Jarman, and most recently Barrett, are illustrating, these 'jolly' classrooms were perhaps more of an adult construct of what a childhood space should be, rather than places that are designed carefully to reflect who we believe the children in our care to be. Common descriptions of Reggio environments are 'light, space, cleanliness, peace, order, nature, commitment, freedom and time' (Hall et al., 2010, p.42). How many adults would like to work in a space that was described in such a way? In that case should it be the same for children?

Team talks and tasks

These quotes could be used as a starting point to discuss as a team (even if that is two of you), prompting thought around who you think children are and what you think about the way that they learn. These are some examples, you will have your own of course. A lovely way to start this activity is to ask each team member to bring along some words that are particularly important to them when describing their work with children.

Creating a shared vision:

> 'Almost all creativity involves purposeful play' (Maslow)
>
> 'Play is the highest form of research' (Einstein)
>
> 'A child loves his play, not because it is easy, but because it is hard' (Dr Spock)
>
> 'I never teach my pupils I only ever provide conditions in which they learn' (Einstein)

So, work together and find out what you share in terms of belief around your philosophical image of a child, how children learn and what the purpose of your

(Continued)

(Continued)

learning environment is. Consider the earlier example whereby we unpicked Malaguzzi's image of a child and applied it to practice. Then search for your philosophy in your environment. For example, if independence is key to your philosophy and pedagogy then how is this fostered in your learning environment? Collaboration is an interesting characteristic to consider, are there spaces to encourage collaboration?

Continuous provision, free flow, levelling areas of learning – what are the implications for your classroom?

There is so much to consider when creating your learning environment, and it is personal, deeply personal. There is advice of course, but this chapter will keep returning to the assertion that there is no one right way. Unfortunately we will not be telling you that you should have certain areas designated in your classroom: should they be organised by subject, skill or experience for example? Do you always need a sand tray in a Reception class? Well, the answer will be found be observing the children. Mr A.B. Clegg regularly asks practitioners to question the usefulness and effectiveness of their 'writing table', among other areas. You can imagine the sharp intakes of breath and complete horror with which this is often met. But his point is correct, look closely at the areas that you have and question how much 'low level learning' is happening. There is a possibility that you have come across Mr Alistair Bryce Clegg (ABC Does); if you have not he is a source of inspiration that all Reception teachers should engage with, listen to, challenge and be 'provoked' by. His passion for the three words 'thrill, will, skill' has become the focus of discussion, debate and change in many Early Years teams across England, and beyond. Both his Twitter account and blog (ABCDoes) are evidence of this. ABC has authority in that he speaks as a Head of an Infants school, where he took on board this approach and made it work. His advice is very real and his vision is clear. He identifies that:

> *Continuous Provision is not 'the provision that is continually out'. It is far more rich and complex than that. If you just put random resources out within your environment then you are relying on a great deal of luck when it comes to children's engagement and attainment. Continuous Provision should 'continue the provision for learning in the absence of an adult'. What I mean by that is the areas of provision you create should be dictated by need, linked to assessment and broadly levelled so that there is challenge and support in all areas for all children.*
>
> (Cited on http://nursery.eastfieldblogs.net)

In order to interpret this and apply it to our own classroom experiences there are underlying factors to consider. Again we are reminded of the central importance of creating a shared vision that is built upon pedagogical discussion as well as sound child development knowledge.

For example, within ABC's quote above there is an inherent assumption regarding play and what 'engagement' and 'attainment' relate to. ABC makes a powerful argument relating to objective-led learning which relates directly to the notion of ensuring that there is adequate 'challenge and support' in all areas for children. It is pertinent to remind ourselves here that pedagogical discussion will be key in identifying whether all members of staff understand and can interpret this. For example, the understanding that all staff will have an objective that will be taken to children where they are learning rather than children being ticked off one by one as they complete an activity. This is an enormous leap for some and needs to be guided and supported. Often discussion helps, as well as observing and finding others who are evolving a similar approach. It is important to turn the abstract into real. (See the team tasks and talks above for examples of quotes and potential discussion points that could help with a pedagogical discussion of this nature.)

Discussing practices in Reggio Emilia, Malaguzzi refers to osmosis as a process to reflect on when discussing what the environment should be, relating to a flow between the outside community and the inside of the school (Edwards et al., 1989). This could be interpreted as giving us strength to remember that our schools should look different. Objective-led planning can be seen as an ideal to aspire to and reflect upon, in order to challenge our own practice. When challenging our own practice we can then ensure that it reflects what is correct for the children and families in our community.

Essentially, our environment is there for a reason and as a team of adults involved in organising and resourcing it we understand what that reason is. The way in which children access the environment we have created for them demonstrates our pedagogy. The following vignette encourages us to question the way in which we, as part of our environment, can fully support, foster and develop children's learning.

Vignette

Self-accessing resources

Many adults set a low expectation that the children will 'just empty everything, everywhere'. This is often not the case with the children hesitant to get resources out for themselves. This requires constant modelling and enabling from the adults, with the adults actively making suggestions, such as 'I know what I could use… masking tape. I know where that is stored in the workshop. Let's go and get some and when we have finished with it we can put it back'. There is also something about encouraging the children to talk about their 'purpose'. When observing a child heaping sand on top of a flower bed I enquired, 'What's the plan with the sand?' the child answered, 'I'm having a funeral for the dead fly. He's dead now so we buried him.' This of course led to a sign being created to show where the now dead fly lay and an emotional rendition of 'twinkle, twinkle, little star' being sung around his little grave. In a setting where 'the sand is not taken from the sand pit' the child could not have played with these big feelings in a safe environment. I also would not have learned how this child understood life and death and the deep empathy that she held.

Point to ponder

What are the features of this enabling environment that has supported this child? What was the adult role in supporting this opportunity?

Choosing when to dedicate this time and energy into one 'thread' of play can be tricky. As discussed earlier this is often instinctive but other times the children tell you in other ways. The following vignette seeks to demonstrate how a thread of play and sustained shared thinking can occur with you as the adult moving in and out of it at certain times. When you 'move out' of the thread of play the learning environment should enable the child to continue and indeed develop their play further.

The story of Caleb's conker will hopefully let you peep through the 'window' into our environment.

Point to ponder

(while reading the vignette below)

How did both the adult and the resources scaffold Caleb's learning? What do you know about Caleb's attitude to learning? How has the environment enabled this attitude?

Vignette

Caleb's conker

Caleb found a conker in the home corner and noticed that it had a crack in it. 'Is it starting to grow?' I wondered aloud. We sat together and had a look on the internet to find out more about what happened when conkers grow. We happened upon a short time lapse clip of conkers germinating. We watched the clip a couple of times before Caleb moved away and went outside. I thought that he had moved onto something else in his play and began helping a child put on their waterproof suit and boots when I overheard another member of staff say to him, 'Caleb, do you need a spade? It might help you to dig a hole'. I realised that Caleb was still working through this 'conker growing' idea and had a plan to plant it himself. I was aware of him digging and planting this conker whilst I was engaged with another child and I heard him say, 'I'll put a stick in to know where it is'. As he looked around for a suitable stick I suggested we made a 'proper plant label'. He responded to this very positively and we went over to the workshop to find the things we needed. We selected a plastic disposable plate as it is waterproof

(Continued)

(Continued)

and we talked about what shape to make it and we decided on a triangle as 'the pointy bit can stick in the ground'. Caleb drew a detailed picture of the broken conker and asked me if I would write the label which should say 'Caleb's broken conker'. The label didn't go into the ground as easily as expected but we solved this problem by digging a little hole and then filling it in with the label in place. Content that the job was complete Caleb moved on to one of his favourite forms of play, pretending that he is a 'power ranger', and I moved on to play with another group of children. Later on I was inside writing with some children in the workshop and Caleb called my name from the outside door requesting that I come outside, saying, 'The conker's grown already!' I shook my head saying that it couldn't have done and I reminded him of the song we sing 'find a little seed, plant it in the ground, wait for it to grow, don't disturb it...'. He continued to insist that I come and see. However, I was really engaged with another group of children so I suggested that Francesca, another member of staff, would love to see what it was. He acquiesced and showed the other member of staff but came straight back, and Francesca commented that he really wanted to show me. I made the decision to leave the group that I had been working with and went outside. Caleb proudly indicated with splayed hand the spot where the conker had been buried. 'It has grown already!' he said, giggling. I feigned shock and surprise as where the conker had been planted there was a conker tucked inside its spiky shell. 'How could this have happened?' 'I speeded it up like they did on the computer,' he announced proudly.

Caleb's conker is an example of an environment that fosters a belief that children and adults can be partners in learning. This belief is based upon a clear, shared vision of childhood and the adults' role within this, as demonstrated by the team work between staff. In addition, the adults involved have an inherent understanding of child development. In Chapter 2, Eleonora expertly explains and challenges our notions of what it is to be four, and we are reminded of the five domains of development: physical, cognitive, language, social and emotional development. These areas of development are inter-related and provide a common base from which we should consider the organisation of the learning spaces that we create for our children:

- *Physical Development:* do they have enough space to move?

- *Cognitive Development:* are there spaces organised in a way that will encourage children to question why?

- *Language Development:* are there spaces for children to talk in a way that suits them? Quiet and cosy space for some, enough space to be with a larger group of friends outside for others … and perhaps a different type of talk.

- *Social and Emotional Development:* is there emotional space for children's resilience to be fostered? Is there time within the routine for children to develop their friendships and can adults support them gently in doing this?

Figure 5.3 Oscar is thrilled to find 'treasure' in the digging area. He is focused for a very long time on finding every piece and placing them in careful lines. This is the beginning of an exciting journey of discovery as we ask him and his friends, where has this treasure come from? How did it get into our digging pit?

Children designing their own environment

If a learning environment is ever-evolving and responding to the adults and children who work within it then this space should be unique. Rinaldi reminds us that, 'the schools in Reggio Emilia could not be just anywhere and no one of them could serve as an exact model to be copied literally elsewhere' (cited in Edwards et al., 1998, p.177). The interests of your class should be the drivers for your environment and the children will be able to share with you their visions of the place they want to learn. The following vignettes show the ideas of a passionate teacher (Claire), mediated by the children she teaches and appropriate to the negotiated pedagogy of her team.

Vignette

A place for everything and everything in its place

Although this is not yet a complete and consistent reality in my setting it is the aim. An organised setting actively supports the learning and the children's autonomy within this. We have created

(Continued)

(Continued)

'zones' or 'spaces' within the four walls of our learning environment; the aim for each space is to be 'readable' for the children. When the children approach the area they know that 'This is a place for… constructing, creating, imagining, etc.'. The children co-construct these spaces with their creations, be they artwork or mark making. During our shared time on the carpet we begin to plan out our learning for this day and if a child has a clear plan of her next project or line of enquiry they can direct themselves to the most appropriate area with very little support. On the other hand a child who has not got a clear sense of what they intend to learn on that day is encouraged to move around the environment to see what provokes their interest. Although the resources are organised into zones there is an expectation that they will be transported around the learning environment. It is our role to enable the children to make choices about what they need for their learning and where may be the best place for that learning to develop. The children's jotters are stored near the carpet area in individual 'wall pockets' but we want the children to take them everywhere! In our setting we find the children are a little reluctant to access resources themselves. Therefore it requires constantly modelling and enabling from the adults. With the adults actively saying such things as, 'I know what I could use… masking tape. I know where that is stored in the workshop. Let's go and get some and when we have finished with it we can put it back.' There is also something about encouraging the children to talk about their 'purpose'.

In the past I have been accused of being a 'hoarder' – this being backed up by the creaking door of the shed which is full of cardboard, packaging, material, wire frames and tubes, to name a few. There is something to be said for having a store of open-ended resources. It is only through having these random objects to hand that we have been able to fulfil the child's ideas in the present. A simple example is of turning the climbing frame into a castle. I could co-construct the castle with the children, planning, overcoming problems and evaluating together. The children continued the basic structure we had made independently. One child disappeared to our 'workshop' and later returned with a full-sized material flag of her own design and creation, which we stuck to the end of the broom and secured to the battlements. Another group transported our foam 'house bricks' to create a soft 'bed' for the king to sleep on underneath the ladder. Another group of children began building their own castle to rival the original building. So much learning and collaboration rippled from the original 'pebble idea' of the castle. All it required was very large boxes, material, the resources in our continuous provision and gaffer tape, lots and lots of gaffer tape!

Over time the children lead this involved and extended interaction with the learning environment, needing less and less guidance from the adults.

In the previous chapter we looked at being a 'collaborator of learning'; however, with the high number of different 'threads of learning' happening at one time within the classroom it would be impossible to be fully immersed in all. This is where the learning environment must take over from you and when created correctly it will not only provoke play but sustain and develop learning.

Vignette

Daily, our little community surprises me. I often take a moment to simply stand and watch them. And it amazes me. The ways that they interact together, look after one another, are engrossed in their learning and move around the environment happy, sure and confident as 'fish in water'. It is a truly special feeling when you have enabled your space to empower your children such as this. There are also a few times where a child or group of children do or say something which challenges your ideas and perceptions. I am grateful for these times as they enable me to align my thoughts about our space closer to theirs. Indeed there are resources within the setting which are 'for the adults' more than the children. It is important to me to communicate with parents, colleagues and visitors our ethos and our learning. Our environment reflects our children and our community. It is vibrant and full of colour as we want our children to be excited and inspired. With another group or in another setting I may decide that my environment needs to be cooler and calmer. These are the choices we make when we design and create a space. Yes there is bunting and a giant watch on the wall, a boat outside and a child-led mural on the slope. I would like to think these things create a 'feeling' within the setting for both the children and any adults as well as providing learning opportunities. However, as an adult we can make mistakes. Here are a few that I have made and without the children feeling ownership and able to challenge me I never would have known.

No netting: I hung out camouflage netting over the mud kitchen and I was very pleased with how it looked. The children were ducking under to mix and concoct with the mud for over two weeks before Caydan questioned 'Why do we have this here?' I replied, 'Oh well, I guess it makes the mud kitchen feel exciting like it is in a den.' Whilst saying this I noticed Caydan's progress toward the water butt to collect water being slowed by being stuck in the netting. 'I wish we could take it down, it gets in the way.' With some regret I began taking the netting down and the bare area no longer looked nearly as exciting. 'That's better,' another child commented and the rest of the group agreed. How long would the netting have stayed up, looking 'inviting' to the adults and a 'barrier to play' for the children? I had misjudged a part of the environment but reassured myself with the fact that the children could challenge me and let me know.

Can we have the climbing frame back?: A different cohort of children and our team had observed the children deeply engaged with water play, particularly with the guttering and tubes. We built a water play station all over the climbing frame. Securing guttering, flower pots, tubes and chutes. The children explored this new space and solved the problems that this presented including climbing and carrying water to drop from the top of the tube. As a team we congratulated ourselves on the learning provocation we had created. A couple of days later a child asked me, 'Can we have the climbing frame back?' and another child said, 'How come it hasn't been tidied away yet?' I explained that we were still exploring the water chutes and tubes. Except as I spoke I realised that I was talking for the collective and making an incorrect assumption. 'We' were no longer exploring the water and even though it had taken time to set up and create I could not ignore the children's request. So we took all the extra resources down and returned them to their stored place.

(Continued)

(Continued)

Figure 5.4 The water station – 'when can we have our climbing frame back?'

Free-space: Yet another mistake has been to overload the number or resources in an area. We may notice that a space is not 'working' as well as would hope, it might be a bit of an 'empty' area. We will have a bit of a move around, removing the resources and moving elsewhere. We will then return to the area to find a group of children deeply engaged in the space with the remaining few resources left behind. Could it be the 'novelty' of the lack of resources or just the open-endedness of the free-space? A change or move around can ignite new interest in a space so it is important that your environment does change and evolve throughout the year reflecting the needs and motivations of your children.

? Point to ponder

When reflecting upon these mistakes that have been made, consider: What has been the ethos of the setting to enable the children to challenge the adults? What do we know about the relationships between the children and adults? How could the views of the children be gathered before amending the environment? I have to ask myself how many other times have I made a 'mistake' without anyone alerting me? All we can do is put ourselves in the place of the child as much as possible. When we are engaged in sustained shared thinking we are using the environment in a child-like way so consider how the environment enables or put up 'barriers'.

Vignette

As mentioned earlier I am grateful to be challenged and impressed when I am held to account. When involving the children in decision making, expect the children to question if something has not been followed through. If we are asking our children to take the risk of suggesting and offering their ideas we must repay them by making them become a reality where possible. During our planning time I had recorded the children's ideas about what we would do and learn following the story of 'the gingerbread man' and we left feeling enthused for the following week. We were about one hour into our morning session on Monday morning when a child approached me saying, 'I thought we were learning about the gingerbread man?' I replied saying that we were! The child then said, 'But we were going to make the puppets where we put our fingers though the holes to make his legs.' I reassured him that we would be doing this on a different day, and that we had the whole week to do all of the things that we had planned. I made sure we had all the things ready to make these puppets the following day.

Vignette

Setting up and using a studio in a Reception class

After having been inspired by Reggio Emilia for quite a few years now I was convinced of the value and significance of the atelier, studio. Always quite envious of the possibilities this would offer I harboured a longing for a space that I could call a studio and set it up in a way that would enable children to see themselves as artists. Joining a new school that had wanted to 'redefine' the Early Years provision I was afforded the very fortunate position of having a spare space in between two classrooms. First, I needed to share this very clear picture I had in my mind. This is the first challenge, whilst exciting it is also daunting to share something that is deeply personal. There is always the possibility that those you want to share with may not agree, understand or simply not 'see' it. I felt strongly at this stage that it was my responsibility to share my picture in such a way that it was clear then, I had to understand that if anybody did not like it then it was my fault for not explaining it properly. So, the journey began with my new team happily reading and looking at lovely images from Reggio Emilia — allowing them time (I hope) to digest the information for themselves. That is only part of the story though as there was a mountain ahead and the climbing of that had to do with us evolving as a team and developing a shared understanding that was not just mine and ours.

Secondly, the children. Once the children started to use the studio it really began to change and evolve. It has become a journey all of its own. We are now in our third year of using the studio and I am happy and proud to say that it looks completely different now to the early stages. Admittedly, there is a collection of clutter, which I struggle with daily, however there is also a sense in this space that it belongs to these children and us.

(Continued)

(Continued)

Thirdly, it is growing as a pedagogical space. At the end of the first year of using the studio Kate, my wonderful teaching assistant, said to me 'that colour wheel needs to go now'. I was horrified as it was a prized possession and I had been so excited about the children's learning that had evolved whilst they were engaged in producing it. So we discussed, debated and she was right it was part of the children's experience and in September we were welcoming new children who were starting a new story with us. The studio was going to be their space. The pedagogical debate continued as at the end of the second year we had another similar situation where the children had created the most inspiring 3D model of the solar system, entirely motivated by their total fascination with all things 'Space'. This time our discussion took a different direction. We were aware of the connection that children felt with this piece of work, which I now look on as an installation that must stay. For now it belongs.

Fourthly, the studio is a space that has fostered and supported transitions. That is transitions for us and children. The children who have left us, return for a sculpture club run for Years 1 and 2. We can see them use the studio in a way that demonstrates their confidence in there. Recently a boy who is now in Year One returned and said 'I remember what we learnt in here, you taught us that if you make a mistake it might be a good thing… the mistake might turn into something good … that we didn't know yet.' He is a marvel and the studio cannot take all of the credit of course! However, it was pure joy to hear him say that and I hope that he uses his deep pocket to take that learning with him into the future.

Figure 5.5 Our solar system

> **? Point to ponder**
>
> Reflect on the five domains of development explored by Eleonora in Chapter 2 and look for signs of them being supported by the enabling environments illustrated in the vignettes in this chapter.
>
> How long should artwork that has been created collaboratively remain on 'display'? Consider the artwork we choose to hang in our own home and work spaces? Do we need to hurriedly remove it every six weeks because our focus has changed?

Conclusion

In concluding this chapter our hope is that you will be inspired to consider the individuality and uniqueness of your classroom space, whatever it may be and whatever stage it may be at. Our classroom spaces are places of wonder and they should reflect that privilege we feel and share in working with the unique individuals who make up our Reception class. Sources of inspiration should remain as that, not models to follow and reproduce. At the beginning of this chapter we identified Bruner who reminded us that school should be a place where children are *invited to grow in mind, in sensibility and in belonging to a broader community*; this is an aspiration we can all hold true. After all, consider the studio space that Joan Miró used in Majorca in comparison to that of Barbara Hepworth in St Ives, Cornwall. Both could be described as artistic geniuses, both needing entirely different spaces to be inspired but born out of the entirely different communities to which they belonged. There must have been similarities in the tools that they needed and to some extent the ways in which these may have been organised, but ultimately they needed spaces that fostered their creativity and as a result produced brilliance.

> **? Point to ponder**
>
> If the hundred languages of expression exist, how does my environment support the communication of them? As an Early Years team do we share an understanding of what purpose our environment has? Can a staff meeting/team meeting be focused on the environment? (Use the list of quotes and ideas about the environment as a prompt for discussion.) Have I reminded myself that this is going to take time?

Further inspiration

ABCDoes

http://www.abcdoes.com/abc-does-a-blog/2014/11/3-little-words-i-am-longing-to-hear-thrill-will-skill/

Elizabeth Jarman and Communication Friendly Spaces

http://www.elizabethjarmantraining.co.uk

Tishy Lishy, is on Facebook, Twitter, Pinterest and there is a blog. Bursting with gorgeous Early Years ideas and generously shared photographs of her inspiring environment regularly:

http://tishylishy.co.uk

Community Playthings: long standing and highly respected within the sector for beautiful and thoughtful furniture as well as resources. Their website is a wonderful source of inspiration, a 'Learning Library' that houses a wide range of theoretical and practical articles as well as a wealth of free resources which can be used to explain many of the points covered in this chapter.

http://www.communityplaythings.co.uk

References

Barrett, L. (2015) *Clever classrooms*. University of Salford.

Bruner, J. (1997) *The culture of education*. Boston, MA: Harvard University Press.

DfES (2012) *The Early Years Foundations Stage* (EYFS). Runcorn: DfES.

Edwards, C., Gandini, L. and Forman, G. (Eds) (1998) *The hundred languages of children (2nd ed.)*. New York: Ablex Publishing.

Hall, K., Horgan, M., Ridgway,A., Murphy,R., Cunneen, M. and Cunningham, D. (2014) *Loris Malaguzzi and the Reggio Emilia approach*. London: Bloomsbury.

Penn, H. (1997) *Comparing nurseries: Staff and children in Italy, Spain and the UK*. London: Paul Chapman Publishing.

Rinaldi, C. (2005) 'Documentation and assessment: What is the relationship?', in A. Clark, A. Kjørholt and P. Moss (Eds) *Beyond listening: Children's perspectives on early childhood services*. Bristol: Policy Press.

Thornton, L. and Brunton, P. (2007) *Understanding the Reggio Approach (2nd ed.)*. London: David Fulton Publishing.

Jottings

6 You as a landscape architect

Gillian Sykes

In this chapter we will begin to consider:

- what we mean by a Reception teacher's likeness to a 'landscape architect';
- how personal influences shape what we do in the outdoors;
- the historical and cultural context of outdoor learning and how this may influence our practice;
- current and contemporary ideas for the outdoors;
- the benefits of the outdoors to young children's holistic development;
- how these aspects then help us to design rich outdoor environments.

Introduction

Why you might ask have we used the heading 'You as a landscape architect'? Well, if we look at the role description of a landscape architect we can begin to see many parallels to that of a Reception teacher. Landscape architects are described as creating the landscape around us. They plan, design and manage open spaces including both natural and built environments. How does this translate into our role as a Reception teacher? Depending on the location of your school, a Reception teacher is often faced with an outdoor area which needs some planning and design to make it effective for the young children who will access it on a daily basis.

A landscape architect works to provide innovative and aesthetically pleasing environments for people to enjoy, while ensuring that changes to the natural environment are appropriate, sensitive and sustainable. A Reception teacher works in much the same way. An outdoor area for young children should be exciting and enticing, building on the important aspect of 'nature' and the 'unique qualities of the outdoors'. It should be planned to remain accessible, appealing and safe for the young learners who freely access it. The changes, through the seasons and weather, should enhance the area creating a diverse, changeable learning environment.

The work of a landscape architect covers diverse projects – both urban and rural. Isn't this also the case for a Reception teacher? For some, you will be faced with a Victorian school playground with large concrete expanses and high walls, while others will enjoy the freedom of fields and trees. However, regardless of location, a Reception teacher works determinedly to provide the best outdoor facilities possible.

A landscape architect collaborates closely with landscape contractors, as well as other professionals. This is an interesting consideration as our main contractors should be the children we are working with, and the other professionals would be our colleagues and those we can persuade and prevail upon to support the development of our outdoor areas. At times, this calls for some creative thinking and a certain amount of 'sweet-talking'.

These aspects will form the foundations of this chapter. However, it will be based on the premise of this well-respected quote from Margaret McMillan in the early 1900s: 'The best classroom and the widest cupboard is roofed only by the sky'. Although this quote is now widely used, I make no apologies for applying it here, as its sentiments are perfect to form the essence of this chapter.

Setting the context – reflecting on personal key influences and inspiration

When I offered to write this chapter, I began to reflect back over my career as a Reception teacher. I began to deliberate on my particular journey as a Reception teacher, having taught in different schools, across a range of local authorities. What had been the key influences that had developed a personal pedagogy so clearly drawn to the outdoors? How did, or do, I know that the 'outdoors' is vital to young children's learning and development?

Team talks and tasks

While reading my personal reflections on the importance of the outdoors to young children you might like to begin to consider your own journey and how this has influenced your own pedagogy. Use your reflections to begin a staff meeting where you encourage staff to begin to think back to their own outdoor memories.

My childhood in the 1960s and 1970s was a happy one. Much of my leisure time was spent outdoors. I can call to mind a worm hospital which I lovingly set up with my sister to care for worms cut in half by my dad's spade. At other times, we explored the rambling glen behind our house, galloping around on pretend horses and escaping from the 'baddies'. Or just out walking in the glorious Yorkshire countryside, in all weathers, with family and friends. In time I became a brownie, girl guide and then climbed to the heady heights of a being a ranger. This involved camping, hiking and generally having fun. I learnt how to take risks, understand about nature and developed a quiet confidence, independence and 'sense of self'.

Having started my teacher training (3–8 year olds) in 1979 it is difficult to remember much of what I was taught or indeed learnt. However, I do remember a lecturer who would take us 'out and about' in a much-loved module called 'environmental studies'. He also took us on a residential trip to Boggle Hole on the North Yorkshire Coast, where we stayed in a rather bleak, grey, smelly youth hostel. This said, I still have vivid memories of rock pooling and hunting for fossils, amidst laughter and wet feet. While the importance of the outdoors was not made explicit in my training, we were introduced to the importance of physical development, experiential learning and to some of the great pioneers who have influenced Early Years education today.

Teaching practices were again in a range of schools. The outdoors was used mainly at playtimes as a means of 'letting off steam', and was less to do with planned teaching and learning. Indeed, for many teachers, and student teachers, the idea of 'playground duty' was one which filled them with horror; sorting out grazed knees, over-exuberant play and tearful little souls who had no one to play with. Worse still was making your way to the staff room for a coffee, and feeling sorry for the rows of children outside the head teacher's office who had not conformed in class. Even as a young student teacher, my heart would go out to these children, and I knew instinctively that the freedom of the outdoors would have improved their behaviour and concentration. Yet, intuition is not always enough, and certainly not as a student. I needed something concrete on which to base my beliefs.

My first teaching post was as a Reception teacher in a small village school. As '4+' education was new to this particular county I was fortunate to attend training to ensure that these young children received an appropriate Early Years curriculum. This appeared to be the stage when I could really begin to apply theory to practice as I was introduced to some of the key pioneers who put outdoor learning on the 'Early Years map'.

It is hoped that by reading this chapter you will begin to challenge and question your own practice. The pioneers discussed here were recognised for trying to alter the 'status quo' and for challenging prevailing views and opinions. Without being able to reflect upon the past, we would be unable to think about the present.

> **? Point to ponder**
>
> What personal experiences have influenced what you do/seek to do in the outdoors? Can you identify key inspirations for the importance of providing effective outdoor provision for Reception children?

The historical and cultural context

It would be pointless to begin to look at the Reception teachers' roles in providing children with access to the outdoors without first placing it in its historical and cultural context. Across the ages there has been considerable interest in the value of the outdoors to young children's learning. Unlike the changing landscape of opinion on the indoor environment (see Chapter 5), Early Years' pioneers have generally agreed that the outdoors is beneficial to young children's learning. Here we refer to the likes of Rousseau and Pestalozzi, Froebel and McMillan and the influence they had in shaping the use of the outdoors in Early Years education across Europe.

Friedrich Froebel (1782–1852) was born in Thuringia, now part of Germany, and was greatly influenced by the Swiss philosopher Rousseau, and Swiss educator Pestalozzi. Rousseau, although a controversial figure, believed that children should be allowed to be children, and should be closer to nature. In a similar vein Pestalozzi saw how much happier children in the countryside appeared to be, compared with their counterparts in 'towns'. He noted how once children started school they appeared to lose their enthusiasm and energy. He believed that education must be according with nature and wrote that a loving and secure environment was the foundation on which learning was built. Influenced by these 'thinkers' Froebel has become well known for his view that play is children's work. He also placed an emphasis on combining play and the outdoors. His philosophy of education saw the introduction of metaphorical and literal 'gardens for children', now known as Kindergartens. Adults nurtured children's development as a gardener would nurture their plants. Through these Froebelian Kindergartens young children were given the freedom to enjoy nature and the outdoors, and were provided with space to garden. Froebel's love of plants and his own apprenticeship as a forester was reflected in the value he placed in nature. Walks within the natural environment, and an emphasis on light and space, were key aspects in his recommendations of effective educational practices.

Maria Montessori (1869–1952) further developed Froebel's ideas. She provided a 'children's house' in a deprived area of Rome. The garden for the 'children's house' sat amidst large tenement buildings, and provided a courtyard in which children could play. Due to the climate, this courtyard was bordered with trees to provide much needed shade for the children.

Montessori established individual gardens for the children to maintain and to support independence and a sense of responsibility.

In the UK, in the early 1900s, pioneers Margaret McMillan (1860–1931), a socialist politician, and her sister Rachel, sought to support the poorest children. Their philosophy was based on the premise that health and education are inseparable, and that being outdoors made a measurable impact on people's lives. These benefits were especially noteworthy to improving the health and well-being of children. Margaret McMillan's famous quote: 'The best classroom and the widest cupboard is roofed only by the sky' sums up how many Early Years' practitioners now view the outdoors. The McMillan sisters established the first Open Air Nursery in Deptford, London in 1914. This carefully planned children's garden was not 'thrown together', it was thoughtfully organised with the children's interests and needs central to its design (Bilton, 2010). Bilton also notes that the relevance of this work on today's practice is that the planned space helps children to foster a love of nature, promotes healthy physical activity and social inclusion. The real life environment avoids a task-structured environment and offers ever-changing first-hand sensory experiences. Indeed a 'junk heap' provided the richest of play areas, with an abundance of rubbish consisting of for example: stones, sticks, tin cans and old pots. An area where all children would love to construct and explore. A deliberate, considered place where children and adults could play and learn together. The Rachel McMillan nursery school set up in 1917 also placed a strong emphasis on the outdoors. Interestingly the classrooms were called 'shelters', each with their own verandas to give the children access to the outdoors in all weathers. Children were reported as having improved mental and physical well-being. These nurseries have influenced how many Early Years settings have been planned with partially sheltered areas providing access to the outdoors in all weathers.

In much the same way Susan Isaacs (1885–1948) based her educational philosophy on supporting the holistic development of the child. The 'school room' at the famous Malting House in Cambridge, opened on to a garden with a summer house, outside water tap, a place for making bonfires and an unusual see-saw. Here there were opportunities for children to play in sand, to care for animals, grow plants and to climb on the first climbing frame seen in the UK. This was a garden which offered real risk and challenge as children investigated and mended, dug and adventured. Children were encouraged to explore and to be curious, with no fixed curriculum and permission to follow their own interests. Adults were able to really get to know the children, through close observations. Observations of children exhibiting real emotions of anger, wonder and fear. The garden became the safe place to learn how to express and regulate these powerful feelings. Reports were that the children at Malting House School learnt how to regulate their own behaviour and were seen in deep concentration developing their sense and knowledge of the world. Isaac's meticulous documentation of the behaviour and thinking of these children challenged, and continues to challenge, the practice of those working with young children.

Two lesser known, but equally important pioneers for outdoor learning, were Professor Carl Sørenson and Marjorie Allen (Lady Allen of Hurtwood). Sørenson, who coincidentally was a landscape architect, developed what was known as the 'junk playground'. This was a result of his observations of children who in their free time enjoyed exploring and playing on bomb sites or construction sites. Sørenson noted that it was at these times that children were at their most creative and imaginative. In response to his findings he began to develop a 'junk playground' which he described as being 'the ugliest; yet for me it is the best and most beautiful of my works' (1951, p.314). Each of Sørenson's junk playgrounds had a 'play leader' whose role was to protect the children's play areas and to prevent outside intrusion. Following a visit to Sørenson's first junk playground Marjorie Allen (1897–1976), another landscape architect and visionary, developed the first adventure playgrounds in the UK. Enabling children to engage in adventurous activity and challenge was central to her philosophy.

Therefore, what can we conclude from this section?

Whether we agree with the different perspectives and philosophies discussed is not the key point. What we must do is to open our minds to what messages these brave and proactive people introduced, and whether these messages are something to underpin our own Reception practice in the twenty-first century.

> **Point to ponder**
>
> Can you see any of these philosophies reflected in your own practice or ideologies? Do you see the outdoors as a 'garden'? Is a garden part of your provision or planned provision? Do you provide 'junk materials' for the children to explore and play with? We now refer to these as 'open-ended resources'. When do you/would you provide opportunities for 'adventure'? Is there a place for this in your practice?

Current and contemporary thinking

In England, prior to the introduction of the Foundation Stage (3–5) in 2000 there was little prominence given to the outdoors. Although there was always an understanding of the benefits of the outdoors, there was little encouragement from the government or regulatory bodies to promote or control its use. As alluded to earlier, often the outdoors was used primarily as a 'playtime' for children to 'let off steam'. However, with the introduction of the Foundation Stage in 2000 and the emphasis it placed on play and independence, practitioners began to develop and use the outdoors to support children's learning. Hence, with the introduction of the Early Years Foundation Stage in 2008 this was greeted, by many, with enthusiasm as it stated as a requirement that quality outdoor experiences should be provided on a daily basis.

Many Local Authorities, based on sound underpinning research, were keen to provide funding for Early Years settings to develop their outdoors. Very quickly, training on the value of the outdoors was offered and Early Years' practitioners began to see how they could provide exciting opportunities outside as well as indoors. Ofsted provided good practice examples of how the outdoors enhances children's learning. Alongside this the Labour government published the 'Learning Outside the Classroom Manifesto' (DfES, 2006). This manifesto is once again gaining momentum as 'character education' rises up the government agenda. As educationalists talk about the key character traits that are pre-requisites for academic success, it is hardly surprising that the Council for Learning outside the Classroom (CLOtC, 2015) are promoting the outdoors. They talk of 'robust evidence about the benefits of learning outside the classroom in helping pupils develop resilience, self-confidence, communication skills and the skills of inquiry and problem solving' (Issue 19, March 2015).

In the UK the strength of attitudes towards young children accessing the outdoors have flowed and ebbed, but the opinion in Northern Europe has remained consistent and has resulted in it becoming a 'cultural norm' (Knight, 2012, cited in Papatheodorou and Moyles). The impact of this on the development of the children in these countries has been significant. Therefore, many countries have adopted this well-respected practice and have recognised that the outdoors should be accessed no matter what the weather. The Norwegian age-old saying 'there is no such thing as bad weather, only wrong clothing' has meant that many Early Years' schools and settings have invested in wellingtons and waterproofs, sunhats and areas of shade to help their children benefit and learn from the outdoors in all weather conditions.

The well-respected Forest School movement, which began in Scandinavia in the 1950s, is now popular in many countries and provides environments for wilder play and the opportunities for children to connect with nature and learn about sustainability. In Scandinavia, well-established cultural links with nature have meant that is customary for young children to often spend more time outdoors than they do indoors. However, Knight (cited in Papatheodorou and Moyles, 2012, p.33) reports concerns that modern living, especially technology, is 'eroding this long standing tradition' and that there is now a conscious effort by Early Years' practitioners in Denmark, Sweden and Norway to continue this effective relationship with the outdoors.

Clearly individual countries have different approaches to teaching four and five year olds. This is sometimes to do with the statutory school starting age and sometimes to do with cultural differences. For many less industrialised countries, children often spend a preponderance of their leisure time outdoors, while in those countries which are the global drivers of commerce children often have a greater relationship with technology. Yet the increase in research-based knowledge and understanding that outdoor play is valuable to young children's development is sweeping the world. In 2005 American writer Richard Louv, wrote his now acclaimed book *The Last Child in the Woods*, and introduced the term 'nature deficit disorder'. In short, the book highlights the effects of 'nature deficit' on our generation of children and adults in terms of obesity, depression and attention disorders. Findings have shown how access to nature can reduce the stress hormone cortisol, increase the immune defence system and increases cerebral blood flow. Interestingly, Japan (a key global driver) has heeded the concerns of a disconnection with the outdoors and introduced the practice of *shinrin-yoku*, or forest bathing. This is a practice now observed by about a quarter of the country.

Keeping abreast of global perspectives of the use of the outdoors for young children opens up other possibilities. For example, in Australia, they now have Bush Schools, which use the distinct qualities of their natural world to enhance children's learning. Beach schools are also now becoming more recognised across the UK and if you work near a beach I would urge you to use this wonderful resource to help children to connect with nature. At the end of this chapter you will find a link to the network 'Children and Nature' which helps you to keep up to date with what is happening in outdoor learning across the globe.

Point to ponder

How do you ensure that children benefit from nature? What do you know about other cultures and their use of the outdoors? How has this influenced what you do? How can you keep up to date with worldwide innovations on the use of the outdoors to young children's learning?

The holistic nature of the outdoors in supporting children's development

In Chapter 2, Eleonora introduced us to the concept of what it is like to be a four or five year old and what developmental characteristics we need to be aware of as Reception teachers. These developmental characteristics should underpin what we do in the outdoors, and also what we offer.

This section will investigate how the outdoors can support children's holistic development.

Point to ponder

What then are the benefits and advantages of the outdoors to young children and their learning and development?

In Chapter 2 Eleonora talked of all areas of development – social, emotional, language, cognitive, physical – being interconnected and influencing one another. This is what we would refer to as holistic development.

Vignette

Read this short vignette and note which areas of development (mentioned above) Eliot was demonstrating in his play.

Eliot was seen using a metal spoon to dig a hole in our grassed area. On seeing this I asked what he was doing. He was quick to tell me that he was making a swimming pool. On hearing this a group of interested friends joined Eliot. Gathering momentum Eliot organised this group of eager volunteers to fetch digging equipment and quickly the swimming pool grew in size. 'What else will you need?' I asked. Eliot looked at me scathingly, 'Water, of course.' Once again he sent his friends off to get some water from the outdoor water tap. On pouring the water into the hole the water disappeared. All the children looked at Eliot for reassurance. 'Oh golly!', I said 'What are you going to do?' Eliot asked if I had any plastic. As I looked at him his face lit up. He asked if he could get a plastic carrier bag from the kitchen. Off he went and came back with a bag which he laid in the swimming pool. 'Why have you done that, Eliot?' asked his buddy Jake. 'Because it is waterproof and the water won't be able to go through it.' Eliot then went to get a large bucket of water which he poured very carefully onto the carrier bag. As the carrier bag began to move Eliot, with his group of supporters, decided together, to

Figure 6.1 Eliot and his friends playing with the finished swimming pool

(Continued)

(Continued)

collect some small boulders which were used to weigh down the sides of the plastic. On collecting some small figures they played happily, constructing a diving board and imagining many different scenarios. Mums and dads were shown their construction at the end of the day and Eliot wrote a sign which warned little people of the possible dangers.

Eliot clearly showed the ability to relate confidently with his peers (social development), and he showed the ability to self-regulate (emotional development). Shonkoff and Phillips (2000) define self-regulation as a child's ability to gain control of bodily functions, manage powerful emotions, and maintain focus and attention, clearly exemplified in Eliot's behaviours. Throughout Eliot showed resilience and persistence which Ripley (2013) states matter more to children's life chances than for example, self-esteem. His use of language and vocabulary was also well developed as he described the use of the plastic carrier bag. He used both fine and gross motor skills (physical development) using muscles to dig and carry, developing body sense, control and management through what White (2015, p.30) describes as the sense of proprioception (meaning perception of the self). The challenge of carrying a heavy bucket of water and cobbles from one space to another supporting the development of neurological systems. Cognition development was also demonstrated as he thought through his ideas, connecting prior learning to construct new learning with his peers. This was a fine example of holistic learning that was generated through a child's natural curiosity and interest. Had I been a Reception teacher who had felt the need to direct all learning, this wonderful opportunity would have been missed. Indeed, had I been a Reception teacher where learning was confined to the indoors Eliot would never have found the small divot in our grassed area which laid the seed for his fabulous idea.

So, unsurprisingly we are very aware that the outdoors holds untold benefits for children's development. But as always we may need research to justify to other colleagues, governors and parents the importance of the outdoors. The National Trust publication *Natural Childhood* (Moss, 2012) outlines other benefits and advantages of the outdoors to children's learning. Moss puts these into four categories: health, education, communities and the environment.

Point to ponder

As a Reception teacher you might like to use Moss's categories to justify your decision to take children outdoors. Become strong in your understanding of the value of the outdoors and have applications to practice, which can further validate your views and opinions to others.

Below I have tried to summarise some of Moss's key points and then to suggest what this might look like in the realms of a Reception class.

The health benefits are both physical and mental. Childhood obesity continues to be a problem in our 'digitally enhanced' western society. Therefore, when children play outside they are generally more active for longer periods of time. Enjoyment of the outdoors as a child lays the foundations for the habits of adults. It is commonly agreed that physical activity supports mental well-being. Exposure to nature also reduces stress and aggressive behaviour. One study reported that children suffering from Attention Deficit Hyperactivity Disorder (ADHD) were observed as being three times calmer when they spent time outdoors. Moreover, a recent survey by the National Trust reported that 80 per cent of the happiest people in the UK spent time outdoors.

One year I distinctly remember having a larger than average cohort of boys. In fact 20 of the 28 in the group were rather lively boys! Within a very short space of time we realised that we needed to take our teaching and learning outdoors. This wasn't just for the children's physical and mental well-being, but also for the adults. Giving these children the opportunity to be physical meant that we could also enjoy periods of calm. Our observations were intriguing that year as we watched them racing up and down, transporting huge tyres across large expanses of playground, laying drain pipes and ramps to see which cars moved the fastest and delivering pizzas at a 100 miles an hour to hungry friends. Interestingly I have since found out that one of these little boys shown in the photograph is training to become a doctor and the other an engineer.

This would confirm Sigman's view (2007) where he found that exposure to nature meant that children were more able to concentrate, had better self-discipline, achieved higher in academic studies and had improved awareness and behaviour. They understood more, felt better, and were able to work more cooperatively and were physically healthier. Nature is indeed a wonderful thing.

Figure 6.2 Transporting tyres

In relation to the benefits of the community, Whyte (2007) writes of the importance of personal geographies and relationships with the local environment to help young children develop a sense of citizenship, belonging and wonder. Children need to have a sense and understanding of their world to enable them to make connections with the wider world. Visits to the local community give children opportunities to observe and ask questions regarding the environment and to develop positive and negative attitudes of the things they like and dislike. This also gives you, as Reception teachers, the opportunity to challenge some of the preconceived ideas some children may have. This is especially important for many of the children in schools whose first home may not be within the community where they are educated, for example refugees. By visiting and interacting with the local environment of their school they can begin to develop these important, transferable skills, and understand about respect and the value of diverse communities.

I remember with affection planning with the children who were interested in learning about food. Having asked what they would like to do the children came up with wonderful ideas, for example: going on a picnic, going to the chip shop, going camping and having beans and sausages and so their ideas grew and grew. Needless to say we endeavoured to meet all their ideas and became a very familiar sight in the local community as we visited the supermarket to buy our produce, sat in the park eating our carefully prepared picnic and queued up outside the chip shop waiting eagerly to buy our cone of chips. The children became skilful communicators, eager to keep their environment tidy and to share their adventures with their family and friends. We even managed to erect a tent on the school field and cook sausages and beans. These children came from diverse backgrounds but through interacting with their local community they developed a mutual understanding of what it meant to be a member of that community.

The final category identified by Moss (2012) is the environmental benefits that come with children accessing the outdoors. David Attenborough said '*No one will protect what they do not care about; and no one will care about what they have never experienced*'. This simple, yet profound statement clearly asserts that unless children know about and experience natural history then they will have no regard for safeguarding it for the future.

At this juncture I need to introduce you to Thomas. Thomas was a quiet, rather serious little boy. He wasn't one to chase around the playground, but instead was very curious. Whenever I use the word 'curious' I am reminded of Einstein's quote, 'I am neither very clever nor especially gifted. I am only very, very curious'. This is how I would have described Thomas. He taught us all so much about the natural world. At four years old he could name many birds and we would often call on his skills to help us identify a bird we had seen. His friends were so impressed that we set up a bird hide and the children would take out binoculars and clip boards to look for birds. We would also feed them, draw them and we used books to research more. Under the close supervision of our very own expert Thomas, we had a sculptor carve a wooden owl for our garden, which became the character for many stories and much role play.

Keen to care for our birds we made our own rather wonky, but much-loved bird table. To show how we further safeguarded our natural world we also held a garden party to raise money for the RSPB. With parents, families and the rest of school attending we certainly made 'bird watching' something valuable and exciting. David Attenborough would have been proud of our endeavours.

Figure 6.3 Bird-watching in all weathers

Team talks and tasks

Use the quotes below from Danks and Schofield (2005) as discussion starters within your teams or network of schools. You might also consider using them with governors or parents.

'Young children have a real affinity with the natural world, an insatiable curiosity and a sense of wonder' (p.13)

'Playing outdoors should be a fundamental part of childhood, yet we are in danger of tidying our children away in stuffy bedrooms' (p.12)

'To fully appreciate the diversity of nature, we need to explore it in as many ways as we can' (p.16)

Risk benefits

However, one of the main challenges for us as Reception teachers in using the outdoors confidently with young children is the aspect of risk. Lindon (2011) reminds us that we need to take a responsible approach to risk. Our current English 'Early Years Statutory Guidance' (2014) very rightly places an emphasis on safeguarding young children. However, it is worth noting that Lord Young's 'Common Sense – Common Safety' report (2010) advises the government to take a risk benefit approach to analysis of risk. We must remember that unless children are faced with risks how will they understand or learn how to deal with them (Sykes in Cox and Tarry, 2015). Instead of being risk averse Gill (2009, p.76) suggests that we provide 'children friendly communities' and 'reject what might be called the philosophy of protection and instead adopt a philosophy of resilience'.

Team talks and tasks

There are now 'risk benefit assessment tools' which can be found and downloaded from Tim Gill's thought-provoking website http:// rethinkingchildhood.com. You and your team might find this a useful first step to analysing risk in your school. It is important that you work as a team to ensure that there is consistency in views and approaches. It would be unfair to children for one adult to encourage safe risk taking and another to dissuade it. This website also provides ideas for justifying to over-anxious parents the advantages of accessing the outdoors (more of this in Chapter 8).

So, what do we know of children's understanding of safety at four and five years of age? If children have had a range of experiences and are at the expected stage of development in physical skills then they will be beginning to tackle tasks which require good hand–eye coordination and attention to what they are doing (Lindon, 2011). Therefore it is important that we do not limit children's adventurous activities by our own insecurities and anxieties. We need to facilitate children in developing their ability to risk assess. Remember that there will always be some minor accidents and near misses, but it is our response to these we need to monitor and reflect upon. Lindon (2011, p.19) bullet points four common-sense approaches to supporting children in taking and assessing risk.

- *Use calm words, with useful verbal prompts such as, 'Watch carefully where you put your feet' or 'Please sit and finish your sandwich, and then you can run about'*. Adding a reason will justify your comment and help the children to learn. For example, 'Please sit and finish your sandwich, and then you can run about, otherwise you might choke'.

- *Offer a hand to a child balancing on a low wall or on an obstacle course and let them decide if they need this support. When a less sure child decides to go it alone, they deserve a, 'Well done! You don't need my helping hand anymore'.*

- *Consider being honest with children when it's you who is uneasy. It might be as simple as, 'Just for my sake, please check where you're going to land before you're in mid-air'.*

- *Considerate adults are willing to reflect on their own swift actions. Bad habits can develop of saying, 'No you can't do that!' or 'Stop it right now!' before even considering the genuine level of danger.* I have found myself apologising to children for my lack of confidence in their ability. Children value this approach and understand that we are only human. Honesty tends to be the best policy.

Team talks and tasks

Make peer observations of how you approach children's risk taking. Are you adopting similar approaches? How can you offer each other further support?

Vignette

As you read this vignette, consider how you would have approached this problem.

Although we had our own Early Years outdoor area we were also lucky and had a huge playing field surrounded by trees and bushes. A real wild area. These bushes provided perfect hiding places for the children and they would spend enjoyable playtimes role playing. Unfortunately one boy in Key Stage 1 got a nasty scratch on his face from one of the bushes. His parent approached school showing concern, especially as the scratch was so close to her son's eye. As a knee jerk reaction to this the school decided, in a staff meeting, to stop the children playing in the bushes. As the Reception teacher, my alternate views were understood but disregarded as we needed to be seen to be safeguarding the children. This meant all children were disadvantaged.

I could understand the parents' and head teacher's concerns; however, a problem-solving approach needed to be implemented. Once again I refer to the work of Lindon (2011). Lindon suggests a five-step approach which also involves the children and where possible the parents:

Step 1. Enable a full discussion about the nature of the problem.

Step 2. Generate a range of possible answers to 'what could we do about this problem?'

(Continued)

(Continued)

Step 3. Decide on the best solution out of those discussed.

Step 4. Put the proposed solution into action for long enough to see if and how it works.

Step 5. Monitor and evaluate the situation, and discuss again as necessary (pp. 26 and 27).

Had this approach been adopted then the parents would have understood the impact the ban would have on the children, the children's feelings and how the ban would limit the children's opportunities. Had we provided a clear rationale for our use of the bushes and trees for children's learning, then the parents may have understood more. Inclusion in deciding on a solution would have shared the responsibility, and by careful monitoring, evaluation and further discussion we would have shown that we were valuing everyone's views and feelings. Although this democratic approach takes longer, it is a respectful approach that promotes an ethos of caring and respect.

It is important then that children learn to take manageable risks and learn how to assess risk levels for themselves. How else will children learn how to stay safe in life, and to take risks?

'Life is full of risk, so the best way to prepare children for life is to ensure that they understand how to judge risk for themselves' (Danks and Schofield, 2005, p.15). We can all bring to mind successful people who have been risk takers. As a Reception teacher our role is to have conversations with children about safety issues and to actively listen to their views and opinions. Opening up these dialogues help to bring risk assessing to the forefront, and helps children to take manageable risks. It might mean that we should join in with children's play and adventures helping them to learn how to climb safely or which plants to avoid, and providing them with knowledge to stay safe. Or, it might mean letting them make a few mistakes to learn to be more careful next time. We have all suffered a grazed knee, grass cut or nettle sting. The important thing was we had someone close by to provide reassurance and an explanation to why it happened and how to prevent it happening again.

We cannot and should not take risk away from children. Children will seek adventure and risk taking in secret if we do not allow them to become risk managers. It is at these times that we are not safeguarding our children.

Environments – and your identity as a landscape architect

We have considered the theory behind a Reception teacher providing children with access to the outdoors and have started to build a good rationale for the benefits it can provide. We know the outdoors offers a uniqueness which cannot be replicated in the indoors. Where else can children experience:

- what snow feels like as it falls upon your face;

- the joy of turning a rock to unearth a cluster of mini beasts;

- the potential of a long, knobbly stick;

- the varying properties of mud;

- collecting an abundance of conkers, acorns or leaves;

- making a nest out of freshly cut grass;

- cooking on an open fire;

- running and running and running;

- shouting as loud as you want to;

- standing in the rain under a large umbrella.

Figure 6.4 Standing in the rain under a large umbrella

So, we have agreed that there are untold benefits for children accessing the outdoors. What then do we think our outdoor environments should look like and what experiences can they offer? Consideration should also be given to the value of the local community and planning should seek to utilise this valuable resource. In this section we will look at planning an outdoor environment which I like to refer to as the 'garden'.

Point to ponder

When you plan for learning do you naturally lean towards the indoors rather than the outdoors? Or are you planning for both opportunities?

Your outdoor environments will all be very different and as suggested at the beginning of this chapter will reflect the context in which your young children play, learn and develop. There will be a range of influencing factors: space available, availability of natural materials, risk benefit assessments, children's views and ideas, budgets and so the list could go on (Sykes, in Cox and Tarry, 2015).

A key consideration must be the importance of space to enable children to move. We know that physical development is probably the most important aspect of child development as it is movement that helps the brain to develop. Sally Goddard Blythe (2004) cites Karl Lange who believes that the knowledge a child acquires before the age of six exceeds anything they might learn at university. This is explained by the plasticity of nerve cells. Goddard Blythe (2004) believes that the mind is the product of the brain and the body. She states that life is synonymous with movement, and when we teach the body we also nourish the brain by maintaining neural connections. In short, for good development to occur we need to ensure that we feed the body and mind. We need to see the body as a source of information as everything is learned through the body and its seven sensory systems. The outdoors provides the perfect environment to develop these systems of: balance, proprioception, touch, vision, hearing, taste and smell and to support neurological organisation. Lack of space constrains learning, and this is especially true for young boys. The smallest outdoor space can seem much larger than a small indoor space as the sky is its ceiling. However, when the indoors and outdoors are used in conjunction they become a reasonably sized space (Bilton, 2010). Therefore, direct access to the outdoors through large sliding doors is preferential.

Yet too much open, sterile space can result in children's play lacking depth, and the play becoming overly boisterous. In these instances, it is important that we consider how we can make our environments more engaging and more like the adventure playgrounds introduced by the pioneers Sørenson and Allen (referred to earlier in this chapter). If we think about our outdoors as a garden we can begin to plan for different aspects, and for different purposes. It is now we can think back to the title of this chapter as we refer to the Reception teacher as a landscape architect.

Point to ponder

How can you plan, design and manage your outdoor space making it as natural as possible? How can you provide innovative and aesthetically pleasing environments for your children and families to enjoy, while ensuring that changes to the natural environment are appropriate, sensitive and sustainable? How as a Reception teacher, can you tackle diverse projects – both urban and rural? Who do you need to collaborate with?

It is clear that nothing can or should be done in isolation. The best Reception garden I have seen was developed as an on-going project, and was constantly being transformed. It was designed through close observations of the children's preferences and interests and took their views and opinions into consideration. Having a very small budget the teacher relied on fund raising and the support of the children's families and friends. Bids were written to appeal for grants, and sent to local businesses and charitable organisations. The children became skilled at writing for a purpose as they sent pictures and plans of ideas for their garden, and asked for help in putting their ideas into reality. Over time the garden had a large beach area built, a wild area for adventures and exploration, a garden for growing vegetables and flowers, a multi-sensory garden for quiet and contemplation. It had different levels and different natural surfaces. Projects arose through children's interests and the children contributed to designs and themes. Over the years the garden became weathered and aged. But this only added to its interest and charm.

The outdoor space, Bilton reminds us, needs to be an attractive, stimulating place for learning, full of endless possibilities. Therefore spaces need to be flexible with open-ended potential. Small confined spaces, which can be different things for different children: a den to hide from baddies, a dinosaur world, a secret store or a pizza oven. Larger open areas for: dancing, marching in a band, racing in the Olympics or for building large waterways. We should also be eliciting the views of the children, their parents and the adults in the design of the outdoor space. This fits well with the Mosaic Approach, which is an evaluative technique created by Clark and Moss (2005) and is underpinned by gaining the views of all involved.

Other desired aspects of the garden space are:

- a transitional, partially covered area between the indoors and the outdoors which provides both shade and shelter;

- an outdoor area which has direct vision from the indoors;

- an area for continuous provision;

- an area to 'let off steam';

- a wilder area to connect and learn from nature;

- different surfaces, levels and slopes;

- seating;

- areas for growing;

- storage areas;

- shrubs and trees local to the area;

- if at all possible a water supply. (Sykes, in Cox and Tarry, 2015, p.69)

Having noted the benefits of nature to children's learning then it becomes obvious that we need an environment rich in nature. Natural materials should be utilised which change and mature over time. Fixed, expensive equipment should be avoided as this requires high levels of adult supervision and is limiting in learning potential. If possible, remove plastic equipment, brightly coloured resources, and instead go for attractive natural features and open-ended natural resources.

> ### Team talks and tasks
>
> Research further into the ideas of some of the key pioneers referred to earlier. Choose the elements you deem exciting and which would suit your ethos and action plan as a team to develop your outdoor area. 'Rome was not built in a day' and neither will an effective outdoor area.

Conclusion

We need to do away with the assumption by some 'that knowledge acquired indoors is superior to that gained outside' (Bruce, 1987, p.55 cited in Bilton, 2010, p.36). To do this we need to ensure that we are planning for the outdoors on a daily basis and that we talk of the outdoors at staff meetings. To raise parents' awareness of the importance of the outdoors this needs to be highlighted through all communications: at visits to the school by prospective families, induction meetings, via the school website. Workshops and open days for families should be planned outdoors, and projects could be organised to involve parents in the development of the outdoor facilities (more of this in Chapter 8). The outdoors should feature in training and needs to be recognised as equally valuable to the indoors to encourage a change in mindset.

As a Reception teacher we need to be creative in our thinking and overcome challenges which might prevent children accessing the outdoors. This chapter provides you with a justification to why you should be using the outdoors. Now we need to strive to develop an outdoor environment that is rich and varied. Not only should we see ourselves as land architects, we should also see ourselves as landscape artists where we provide a landscape open to interpretation and choice.

Further inspiration

By signing up to the Children and Nature Network http://www.childrenandnature.org you can be kept up to date with worldwide innovations and research linked to the crucial relationship of nature to young children's development.

Visit a local National Trust site and enquire about how you and your class can become involved in caring for their natural surroundings www.nationaltrust.org.uk

If you are redesigning an outdoor area then consider using the Mosaic Approach (Clark and Moss, 2005) to gather the children's perspectives. Their book *Spaces to play* describes a pilot project and provides inspiration for the development of your outdoor spaces.

Contact the Royal Horticultural Society and join their campaign for school gardening. This has great ideas to inspire and motivate you. https://schoolgardening.rhs.org.uk/home

Access the Learning through Landscapes website at http://www.ltl.org.uk. This website has a space dedicated to transforming outdoor spaces.

Research 'Play Trees'

References

Bilton, H. (2010) *Outdoor learning in the early years: Management and innovation* (3rd ed.). Abingdon: Routledge.

Clark, A. and Moss, P. (2005) *Spaces to play: More listening to young children using the mosaic approach.* London: NCB.

Common Sense – Common safety report (2010) https://www.gov.uk/government/uploads/system/uploads/attachment_data/file/60905/402906_CommonSense_acc.pdf [Accessed 7.1.15].

Council for Learning Outside the Classroom (2015) *Members newsletter.* Issue 19, March 2015.

Cox, A. and Tarry, E. (Eds) (2015) *Playful pedagogies.* Woodbridge: John Catts.

Danks, F. and Schofield, J. (2005) *Nature's playground. London: Frances Lincoln.*

Department for Education and Skills (DfES) (2006) *Learning outside the classroom manifesto.* Nottingham: DfES.

Gill, T. (2009) *No fear: Growing up in a risk averse society.* London: Calouste Gulbenkian Foundation.

Goddard Blythe, S. (2004) *The well balanced child: Movement and early learning.* Stroud: Hawthorn Press.

Lindon, J. (2011) *Too safe for their own good? Helping children learn about risk and life skills.* London: NCB.

Louv, R. (2005) *Last child in the woods.* New York: Workman Publishing Company.

Moss, S. (2012) *Natural childhood.* National Trust outdoor.nation@nationaltrust.org.uk [Accessed 11.1.16]

Papatheodorou, T. and Moyles, J. (Eds) (2012) *Cross-cultural perspectives on early childhood.* London: Sage.

Ripley, A. (2013) *The smartest kids in the world: and how they got that way.* New York: Simon and Schuster.

Shonkoff, J. and Phillips, D. (Eds) (2000) *From neurons to neighborhoods: The science of early childhood development.* A report of the National Research Council. Washington, DC: National Academies Press.

Sigman, A. (2007) *Agricultural literacy: Giving concrete children food for thought.* www.face-online.org.uk/resources/news/Agricultural%20Literacy.pdf [Accessed 3.4.15].

Sørensen, C. T. (1951). Junk playgrounds. Danish Outlook.

White, J. (2015) *Every child a mover.* London: The British Association for Early Childhood Education.

Whyte, T. (2007) Personal geographies – children and their local environment, in R. Austin (Ed.) (2007) *Letting the outside in: developing teaching and learning beyond the early years classroom.* Stoke on Trent: Trentham Books Ltd.

Jottings

7 You as an auditor of children's learning

Shona Lewis and Julia Beckreck

In this chapter we will begin to consider:

- the theory and practice of assessment 'for' and 'of' learning;
- setting the context for observation and assessment;
- the complexities of the assessment process;
- how to observe and assess and the importance of valuing all perspectives;
- observation and assessment 'for' children.

Introduction

We see children's development by what they do. They construct their own learning. Yet how do we observe, understand and respond? In this chapter we consider how adult perceptions and beliefs can impact on what we think children can do. The importance of observing children is highlighted and some strategies and tools suggested. We will look at the influence of theorists and historical pioneers on what we mean by young children's learning. We will also look at more modern day influences including the need for 'data'. Finally we will consider how to interpret and analyse what we see and, most importantly, on how to put our understanding to good use in order to develop children's learning and our teaching.

Figure 7.1 overleaf provides a good shorthand summary of observation, assessment and planning in Reception classes.

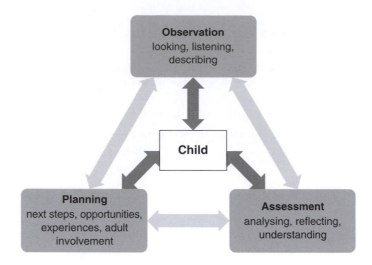

Figure 7.1 Using observation, assessment and planning to support children's individual learning

(adapted from Carter and Nutbrown, 2010, p.19)

For the purposes of this chapter, Nutbrown's cycle has been adapted to highlight the importance of including the child's perspective in:

- making sense of observations;

- informing assessments;

- and then involving them in the planning of further learning opportunities.

The arrows have been changed to go in both directions, as we acknowledge that this cycle is never quite straightforward. For example, sometimes we go back to the observations we have made to gain the views and opinions of our colleagues or parents. Or we might plan learning in a variety of different ways before we make our observations, or we instantly assess the learning.

Before moving on it would be useful to define the two types of assessment that will be referred to in this chapter: assessment *for* learning and assessment *of* learning. Assessment for learning or formative assessment is what you do in your everyday practice when you observe children. Assessment of learning or summative assessment gives you a summary of a child's development at a particular point in time so that progress can be tracked.

Clarke (2002, p.2) uses a gardening analogy to define the two types of assessment. She says that if you think of children as plants then the summative assessment is simply measuring their height and number of blooms. She likens formative assessment to the garden equivalent of looking to see if the plants need feeding or watering – directly affecting their growth and beauty. This analogy fits well within the ethos of the Early Years. However, by adding a further dimension, that of nurturing by the skilled, knowledgeable gardener (teacher), the plant will develop fully to be the best bloom in show. In much the same way, the child will develop uniquely and holistically to be the best they can be.

Already we have acknowledged that assessing children's learning and understanding is complex; however, it can also be viewed as exacting and exciting. In order to assess with perception and accuracy, you must enter the child's world and explore and learn alongside them. It takes time and enthusiastic energy. Young children are wonderfully open to new ideas, free from the perceptions and limits of adult minds. You must become childlike in that respect, if you hope to gain insight into what each child knows, understands and feels. With such insights you can begin to explore, play and learn alongside children, to support them in making sense of their situations, circumstances and interests.

Understanding how children learn

Children are learning from the very minute they are born. They learn to see, to discriminate, to move about, to feed themselves, to walk, to talk, to sort, to scribble, draw and write without being taught! Look at how this learning takes place, varying with each child. Look at the role of the adult in encouraging and enabling this learning. Look at how we assess, enjoy and record this learning. We must replicate this approach with Reception children.

The concept of a child constructing their own learning is often misunderstood. In the past the concept of free play was equally misunderstood. It was thought to be the idea of liberal teachers and educators that children, left to do what they wanted and when, would learn by themselves all they needed to know. Nothing could be further from the truth. Free play, now understood to be the way in which young children learn most effectively, requires a structured environment, imaginative resourcing and close observation and assessment of their learning.

We have learned over years of teaching that children know what they want to explore and get to know, and do so with excellent concentration and determination. Watch a toddler trying to unwrap and open a parcel, or a three year old trying to ride a bike, or build the highest tower. Strangely, the idea that children need to 'get ready to learn', to be taught to concentrate and sit still or be made to draw and write is one firmly held by educational policy makers. It is little wonder that under such pressure children are not reaching the high levels of skills and creative thought that they have inside them.

Teaching is a creative and dynamic activity, and assessment and dialogue are integral to it. The art of teaching in the past used to conjure up images of children in a formal setting, sitting at tables and chairs and having learning delivered to them. People's perceptions have moved on and teaching and learning in a Reception class is now more engaging, stimulating and diverse that it has been for generations.

Dealing with our own values and beliefs

Ultimately it is the teacher who decides what needs to be assessed and how that will be done. Even though all adults in the classroom are working within the same framework it is the teacher's own values and beliefs which drive this process. As a Reception teacher what do you value? For instance, evidence towards the characteristics of effective learning (DfE, 2012) for one teacher might be that the child sits quietly completing an adult-directed task and showing signs of involvement. Another would look at evidence in child-initiated time when the child has control over their own learning. Children quickly learn what their teachers value and many will conform to these values. As advisory teachers we have observed children, clearly showing characteristics of effective learning, deeply involved in their own play only for an adult to call them over to check whether they can match objects to numerals. Deep-level learning stopped in its tracks! Remember that some children have learnt that the quicker they complete a task the sooner they can go back to real learning and also that they are pleasing the teacher. Others, as we know, will avoid the task.

The same child who has been busily sorting out the number of bricks needed to complete a model in the building area might not be able to complete a paper task but if the teacher had spent time observing the child the observation note would give much richer evidence.

This can be equated to attending a conference or lecture and then discussing it with colleagues. There are so many different perceptions for the same event. We need to be continually aware of this when working with children. Drummond (2003, p.48) argues that

'... if we choose only those aspects of learning of which we approve we lose the opportunity to see more of the picture, to learn more about learning'.

> **? Point to ponder**
>
> With this quotation in mind, think how you would respond to this scenario:
> The girls are sitting outside under the tree looking at books; however, their
> peace is interrupted by a group of boys busily engaged in fantasy play. How would
> you assess the learning that is taking place?

Child development

Understanding why and how young children learn and how learning relates to the stages of development is vitally important when assessing children. It stands to reason that if a child is still working within the mathematical stage of one-to-one correspondence with small numbers you should not be expected to assess whether he can tell you one more or less than a number up to 10. Similarly, if a child has very limited language there is no value in assessing if he can write a sentence.

The Development Matters in the Early Years Foundation Stage document (Early Education, 2012), written by people who fully understood through their research and experience how children grow, learn and develop, is an excellent starting point for students and new teachers. Sadly it has been rather downgraded as guidance for those involved in planning and implementing a successful learning environment for young children. We strongly advise reading it. Discuss it with children and colleagues and use it to test your own observations and ideas. The characteristics of effective learning section in particular is a good place to start as this will give you clear ideas for analysing observations and questioning practice. Child development is very fully addressed in Chapter 2, and this is also an excellent source to develop your understanding.

Why do we observe children?

Dubiel (2014, p.35) sees observations as feeding into and driving learning, teaching and pedagogy. This is a powerful statement that encompasses the principles of assessment by putting the child at the heart of the process. If assessment is to be worthwhile and valuable then it must be integral to teaching and learning and must be informed by observations of children. Observing children is not a new concept. To illustrate this point the section below looks at historical perspectives through focusing on just a few of the great pioneers and theorists of early childhood education (some of whom are also discussed in Chapter 6). Looking at their work can help Reception teachers to reflect on their own observations while recognising the complexity of the process of assessment.

Historical perspectives

Froebel (1782–1852) recognised that the early years were the most important years in a child's life. He believed in the importance of play, learning through the senses and physical activities. He recognised the importance of adults observing children in order to understand their thinking. It was through his careful observations of young children and how they responded to their mother singing to them that he developed finger rhymes and action songs, many of which are still used today.

Susan Isaacs (1885–1948) is another pioneer of early childhood education. The cornerstone of her work was observing children. She believed in the importance of play and providing an environment that stimulated curiosity and catered for the emotional needs of the children. She set up an experimental school in Cambridge and for four years she and her colleagues studied children's learning, documenting this through detailed observations and illustrating how through analysis teachers have a greater understanding of children's intellectual growth and learning. Far from being unstructured as was perceived by some, it was by providing an appropriate environment that her practitioners were able to make such insightful observations into children's learning.

Modern day influences

Margaret Carr, a New Zealand educator, is known for her work in developing learning stories, which are described in a further section. In her writings she also describes the change in her own professional beliefs about assessment. The journey, which has taken her from using assessments to check whether children had acquired the requisite skills for school to her current practice which she calls 'divergent assessment', makes interesting reading. She explains that effective assessment emphasises the learners' understanding and is jointly accomplished by the teacher and the learner.

Read the theories of social constructivism, in particular Vygotsky and Piaget, to help develop your understanding of how they have influenced good Early Years practice today. Although written many years ago, these have rarely been bettered and have sustained us through questioning of our own practice over the years. Being able to justify our practice stands us in good stead as we are bombarded with changing government policies and dictates. We know in our heart that children are capable of wonderful discoveries, of building empathetic relationships and of individual creative thought and practice. They need understanding, creative adults armed with knowledge of their needs and individuality to support and guide them to be truly content and successful people. Sadly, teachers are not always trained now to know how this can be done.

A continuum of learning

It is very useful to think of teaching and learning as one process, one that you share with the children. Your actions, in 'conversation' with the child's actions, can be likened to a dance, each responding to the messages given and received by the other. In this way, with practice and in dialogue with colleagues, you will develop a deeper understanding of all elements of children's learning. Here are some important words to help you during your observational teaching: observation; communication; scaffolding; patterns and schema; play-based learning; sustained shared thinking; relationships and analysis.

Learning to see

Close and frequent observations of children, observations free from predetermined outcomes and adult perceptions are a prerequisite to any assessment that is worthy of the name. What are 'frequent observations'? Observations are an integral part of the Early Years environment and in a Reception classroom we are constantly watching and interacting with children. Many of these observations are not recorded but stored in the memory for future conversations about the children. As a Reception class teacher this is part of your everyday practice and you should never underestimate the importance of this. These are the foundations on which you build the learning and teaching in your classroom.

Vignette

When discussing the power of observations with a former advisory teacher with a wealth of experience of Early Years practice, she said it is something that we do naturally. She went on to recall how in her own Reception class, over 20 years ago, she had noticed a little girl who was very quiet. She was always standing at the edge of activities not really participating. As a result of this observation she set up some small group activities which involved turn taking to help the child feel more confident. She also alerted her staff of the need to be aware of the situation and to model how to join in play. This would not have been documented but was nevertheless a very powerful assessment for learning.

More recently, while spending a morning in a Reception unit a little boy attached himself to me and was keen to work alongside me and talk to me. However, when he was asked to go and explore the environment he found it difficult to engage and kept coming back to me. When I mentioned this to his teacher she said that all the practitioners were aware that this child was finding it difficult and they were trying different ways to encourage him to work with other children. They had observed that he liked deconstructing and had added an old electrical installation and tools to encourage him to work independently. This had been identified on the planning but was not a recorded observation.

To see and understand each child's thought processes, you must watch their behaviour in a variety of situations. Conditions must be set up by the teacher in a way that allows the child to follow his interests and fascinations, with restrictions only on safety and mutual regard in place. A free flow environment where children can make decisions to play and explore both indoors and outdoors, with well-organised and planned activities is essential. These activities must be offered on a daily basis to meet the physical, emotional and intellectual needs of each child in any given class. This means you must look beyond the surface. Look at the situations in which: the child prefers to play alone, talks with peers and/or adults, their energy levels, indicators of well-being, how and when the child makes decisions and so demonstrates interests and preferences. What are you seeing? Often during my discussions with teachers following an observation, we would see quite different things. An outside observer can be free from restrictions imposed by school policies on observation, free from the narrow parameters of any outcomes expected, free from any previous judgements made about that child. Discussions with mentors, advisory teachers and peers can all provide new learning to guide judgements on the quality and depth of the child's real learning for both the teacher and other party. Superficial judgements on what children know are not difficult to make. Adult obsessions with knowledge of colours, numbers, shapes and initial sounds are relatively easy to assess. However, this knowledge can only have any use for children when they fully understand the implications and connections with real life, authentic situations.

In a similar way we should consider problem solving which provides the foundation of a young child's learning. It must be valued, promoted, provided for and sustained. Opportunities for problem solving occur in the everyday context of a child's life. It is during this kind of learning that we must observe and understand in order to further plan and provide opportunities to extend their learning.

Types of observations

Instantaneous, on the spot, magic moments

These are often recorded on post it notes but increasingly on an electronic device with one of a range of assessment tools.

Vignette

The teacher had been playing alongside the children when she observes child A in the building area totally involved in his play. She went over and talked to him about his model and then moved away keeping an eye on developments. She then joined him again later on in the session and continued her conversation with him encouraging him to tell her about the developments to his building. This was obviously a significant moment in child A's learning as she recorded the observation on an electronic assessment tool and then displayed his model in the classroom.

A – spent over 40 minutes working

with the stickle bricks.

When I questioned him he said

it was a house for Percy. He continued

to refine his model adding a chimney.

Date:

This was the first time that A had been concentrating for such an extended period and was constructing with a purpose in mind. How exciting for the teacher. The observation was discussed with colleagues and as a result it was decided to take the maths learning into the construction area as A had difficulties engaging in mathematical activities.

(Continued)

(Continued)

Figure 7.2 A, adding a chimney to his model

Narrative observations

These are detailed and often are planned as a result of needing to know more about the child.

Vignette

The teacher had been concerned about child B's ability to share and was often receiving complaints about B being bossy. The teacher had set up the task, re-enacting the 'Whatever Next' story as part of the continuous provision and then stood back jotting down some significant pointers to enable her to write up the narrative later. Here is an extract:

During an 'explore and learn' session B chose to work outside and quickly started building a spaceship using the large construction with a group of friends. As the spaceship begins to take shape the children start to negotiate who will be in charge of flying it. B quickly takes charge and says ' I will go first and you can fly back when we get home'. Once they had completed the

(Continued)

(Continued)

construction B sits at the front and says, 'I am the driver. Come quickly get on the back, we are going to the moon'. She uses her map to find her route and then says 'It's going to be a long journey'. When the children arrive on the moon they pretend to go outside, collect the props from the story and B suggests they have a picnic. B links her own experience of having a picnic to help her act out the next part of the story. She lays the table and then speaks to baby bear in a small voice, 'Would you like a biscuit or some honey?' After a while B instructs her friends to pack away the picnic things and says, 'Come on, it's time to go home now, you can drive'.

Figure 7.3 The spaceship begins to take shape

The observation was put in B's learning journal with links to the areas of learning. It was shared with other adults in the classroom and then the notes were used at the next planning session to assess the learning and decide next steps in terms of provision and teaching strategies. It was decided to plan more group time activities with adult support to help B to take on a more co-operative role. They would use the interest in space as a starting point.

Tracking

This method of observation is often used to see how a child is accessing the learning environment and to see how involved they are. There are various ways of setting up this observation. In some cases noting down every 15 minutes where the child is working gives a good indication of both involvement and interests.

Vignette

In one school the staff had been concerned that child C found carpet time problematic and also found it difficult to self-regulate in child-initiated activities. They has been watching the child closely and making informal observations but decided to track her to get a better picture. When they came to analyse their observations they were able to clearly see her fascination with sand and how she could sustain concentration when the activity captured her imagination. As a result of this they looked at ways of taking the learning to her, adding more tactile experiences to the learning environment and reconsidered how to reduce the time the children were expected to sit on the carpet.

Going with the children's interests

The easiest way to communicate what is meant by this is with an example.

Vignette

A child had brought in a book about birds to share. Through talking to the child and asking open questions it was clear that the child had a deep interest in birds. The teachers acknowledged her interests and used this to inform the next week's planning. They incorporated a hide in the outside area using camouflage netting and adding binoculars, bird books and clipboards with photos of different birds for the children to identify and record.

Figure 7.4 Involving children in planning their learning

Learning stories

This approach to assessment, developed in New Zealand and described by Carr (1998, 2001, 2004), is an excellent way to find out a child's interests, understandings and stage of development in a wide range of areas of learning. The practice of learning stories is characterised by annotating the stories a child is telling you, be they fact or fiction, then by reading them back, typing them up, seeing them in print, then discussing these stories with the child and perhaps their friends and parents. This supports real understanding and realisations that develop in the child's brain, which then become exciting and dynamic learning. Making a collection of these stories over time for each child will provide a full picture of the development and the significance of each child's unique learning and personality. Alongside video records of a child's day-to-day activities both indoors and outdoors, these recorded stories can be shared with parents, the child and any interested person wishing to assess and understand that child's levels of development and their fascinations.

 Point to ponder

Does current Early Years education policy and practice and assessment methods, provide or deny each child the opportunity to develop creativity and individual talent?

Pedagogical documentation panels or posters

This is a means of documenting episodes of children learning. These are developed with the children and are used to capture their thinking and ideas. Educators from Reggio Emilia see documentation as 'traces' of learning (Wien, 1997) and as 'visible listening' (Rinaldi, 2001, 2006). We can view pedagogical documentation a little like a research story, built upon a question or line of inquiry (Wien, 2011). Educators, children and others develop the research story which requires careful listening and intellectual empathy. It is based on the belief that we will never know the full picture of children's' learning; however, we can wonder and question. We can work cooperatively to develop a representation for just a short glimpse into their world, and then try to develop practice to further support their interests and passions. This would be regarded as assessment 'for' children. Representation which values their thoughts, ideas and theories.

 Team talks and tasks

Conduct your own research into pedagogical documentation. What would work best for your class or group of children?

'An alternative approach'

How and what to observe is not as obvious as these simple questions suggest. In many schools the teacher and/or the subject coordinator decide who is to be observed and then decide what behaviours or knowledge they want to assess against those deemed desirable by the powers that be. This we suggest is a pointless exercise and one that usually has little to do with the child! Teaching and assessment are interchangeable in the Reception class and the two must be happening together all the time in order for you to be effective in challenging the child to further explore and learn.

Here we suggest an alternative approach:

Set up and resource a challenging, exciting activity in one or more areas of learning e.g. literacy development and physical development.

Example A (physical development): Construct a defined play area, either indoors or outdoors or both with an exercise mat, a timer, a skipping rope, rubber stepping stones, low balance beam and a clip board with pre-printed sheets on which the children can record the activity times and success. Also display posters and/or images such as gym advertisements, keep fit advice and healthy eating posters. This play area could be available daily, to be used as the children choose in a free flow, child-initiated learning environment.

Example B (literacy development): Set up a castle interior with puppets and finger puppets of knights, dragons, dressing up armour, cloaks, hats, feathers, etc., a pulley and bucket, brown paper bags, drums and shakers for musical accompaniment. Place carefully selected books e.g. *The paper bag princess* by Robert Munsch, some picture books (those by Babette Cole would work well) on a cushion and leave the rest to the children.

During a period of the day observe the group/groups of children that decide to play in these areas. Write down, or mentally note, who plays in that area, with whom, using which resources and exactly what they do with them. Make a note of any conversations the children engage in. Make a note of any particular interests you observe, by which children and how they are demonstrating those interests. (Only write down what you think you may not remember – try and develop your own shorthand.)

It is important to know how to use these observations, and you need many to get an in-depth picture of what each child knows and can do, as well as how they best learn. The following sections unpick this process.

Strategies to help you assess children's learning
By communication

Communication between adults which promotes understanding and empathy is difficult enough, such communication between adults and young children is even more so.

Communication is a two-way process of equal giving and taking. When communicating with children adults often fail to listen enough. So busy are they directing children what to do, and how and when to do it, that they fail in the crucial aspect of the 'watch' aspect of communication as well as not doing enough listening. Teaching can sometimes get in the way of learning. Nowhere is this more important than when assessing each child's learning.

During observation used as assessing for learning, the everyday and constant role of a teacher, watching and careful listening must become an integral part of the Reception teacher's being. Listening without prejudice and preconception is a difficult skill and can be developed, with practice, in collaboration with colleagues.

By scaffolding

Supporting each child in her learning is the fundamental role of a Reception teacher and part of that role involves scaffolding, a technique described and developed by Vygotsky and Bruner. Briefly, this technique involves offering then giving, should the child accept, just enough support during any given activity, to enable her to acquire a new skill, understanding or insight. A straightforward example of scaffolding could be when a child is attempting to balance along a line or a beam, the adult could walk alongside the child at the child's pace, holding out a hand so that the child can take hold of it if she feels the need to maintain her balance. In this way it will be the child's decision to accept the support or not as she feels the need.

This way of supporting learning can also be successfully used when teaching reading, writing and spelling. For instance, by offering to write, read or spell for a child during a shared activity, it ceases to become a 'test' for the child and becomes mutual learning. The child can then decide whether she needs this support or, that she knows she can do it on her own (as will the adult). In this way each child is enabled to become a confident learner without the anxiety and stress that goes with being tested.

Point to ponder

What is the impact of the current climate of increasing testing on opportunities for meaningful learning in our young children?

By knowing a child's schema

Each person has an individual way of learning and these ways of learning styles must be known and understood by a successful assessor of learning. By close and constant observation of children in their self-chosen play, favourite patterns of play will be seen. There is a body of writing around the notion of schema, most notably Athey (1990), which unpicks the preoccupations we see in children's learning and the patterns of their play. Recognising these means learning activities can then be provided to extend and deepen learning as children are engaged in their continuous self-directed play. The teacher's role is to recognise these patterns and to then engage accordingly with the children to support further learning and development.

By Sustained Shared Thinking

Sustained Shared Thinking was first identified in research associated with the *Effective Provision of Pre-School Education* (EPPE) project in 1992. This term is sometimes shortened to SST and used to describe 'good practice' in interactions between adults and children. It is not always helpfully explained and this has caused some ineffective interpretations.

An explanation that might be clearer is to think of teaching/learning times as a partnership between the child and the teacher, where both are playing, talking and questioning together in order to solve a problem, acquire a new skill or reach a new insight. It is crucial that both participate in this activity equally, both bringing to it seriousness and enjoyment, as well as previous knowledge. Open-ended questions on the part of the teacher will help the child respond uniquely and spontaneously. This enables the teacher to know how to support the child towards a new step in her learning (by an open question we mean one that the questioner does not know the answer to!). It is important to value this approach as leading to a deeper level of learning on the part of both child and teacher.

By play-based learning

There is almost universal acknowledgement that children learn most effectively when they are playing. This can be within an indoor or an outdoor environment but to be effective it must be carefully planned and understood by knowledgeable teachers. That is when significant learning is most likely to take place.

By observing well-being and involvement

Each of us knows that how we are feeling and how alert we are will affect our performance in life, both at home and at work. Research and thinking that is highly recommended, for all those working with young children, was done at Leuven University by Professor Ferre Laevers (2006). He describes stages of well-being in young children and how understanding of this provides knowledge as well as guidelines to help each child reach a high level of learning. The scales of well-being are extremely supportive in helping us understand the emotional and health needs of each child and then planning and providing the appropriate next steps. However, as Laevers points out children need to show high levels of involvement too. Dubiel (2014) likened the characteristics of effective learning to the indicators of child involvement.

? Point to ponder

In your view, is enough credence given to the assessment of children's emotional development and well-being in the Early Years? How do you support well-being in your class?

Figure 7.5 Children feeling emotionally enabled to explore, learn and develop

Analysing learning

Before learning can be recorded it must be analysed. This is done by looking closely, and beyond the obvious, at all the observations made of each child in their play. Observations of children during adult-led activities are more superficial and so less valuable to developing an understanding of the child. Analysis is best done in conversations with colleagues, parents, other professionals and the children themselves. All have much light to shed on the interpretations, learning and understandings of the whole child! An incomplete picture will mean that something crucial about that child will be missed.

Once analysis has been completed and before recording, the plan for next steps in learning must be discussed and the curriculum and/or individual learning plans be reviewed and amended. These will be recorded alongside the learning and stage of development. Gradually a deeper understanding of the child and a knowledge of their achievements is developed to inform teaching.

The importance of including parents

The importance of parents as the prime educator of children was certainly brought to the forefront by the Early Years Foundation Stage framework (2008). This was strengthened, following the Tickell Review of 2010, in the revised EYFS framework (2012, DfE).

The two-way partnership is vital for Reception teachers to put together the whole picture of the child. Some teachers hold the view that parent partnership is about telling the parent how they can help their child at school. However, there is a growing body of belief that there should be a genuine two-way flow of information. This is the way teachers can share what parents and carers know of the child's interests and fascinations and nurture these within the school environment. One of the authors of this chapter still looks back rather shamefacedly at the time of a parents' meeting in the autumn term for her Reception class: '*Child E was a very quiet girl and never really talked much about the books we were sharing. I was amazed to learn from Mum that actually E was reading fluently at home but for some reason did not want to share this at school. What a revelation*'.

Many Reception classes have now put systems in place for parents to share 'wow' moments. These can come in the form of pieces of writing or drawings, comments made or actions observed. Increasingly, technology can enhance the sharing of observations from school and home, and home to school. Many of these are then fed into the school assessment system or added to learning journals.

Point to ponder

How do you involve parents in the home–school learning partnership? Do you think that your partnership with parents is equal?

Have you considered asking parents what they would like their children to learn?

Assessing learning

Assessment involves discussion and explanation between adult and adult, adult and child and between child and child. Ideas and judgements must be explored with others in order to understand how and what learning has taken place. If the assessment is made against a benchmark and/or criteria this must be agreed to be appropriate for the age and stage of the child. In the recent past in England external moderators have worked with Reception teachers in testing and verifying the accuracy of their judgements at the end of the year. This may not continue so it is very important and helpful to carry out internal moderation within your school as well as with others teaching children of Reception age. This can give you a broader perspective as well as reassurance, and will also support validity. Other teachers, parents and above all the children themselves will reveal understanding and insight into each child's learning through moderation of your observations, as well as a child's actual work and conversations. Children love to review their work and creative outpourings, and if you engage with them fully and openly you will both enjoy them and learn more about them as they talk and clarify their thinking.

Whichever government is in office, assessment will always be a tool to quantify or qualify attainment for our children. In the world of increasing accountability, record keeping for accountability can overtake assessment for learning. Hopefully reading this chapter will help you to keep the right balance. Nutbrown (2006) refers to three different purposes for assessment: Assessment for teaching and learning; assessment for management and accountability; and assessment for research. While this chapter is mainly concerned with assessment for teaching and learning it is worth investigating the different recording systems which provide information for management and accountability.

There are a number of possible audiences for assessment:

- for national statistics and government scrutiny;

- for school senior management staff. Individual recording of progress in all areas of learning will enable them to determine the effectiveness of their Early Years provision and to identify areas for development;

- for individual teachers and support staff. Here more detailed notes and written evidence of observations (perhaps in electronic form) will help them understand what and how each child is learning and hence what next experiences and learning activities they must plan;

- for parents and carers. A journal-style record of photos, videos, children's work, and scribed examples of their conversations, including contributions from parents;

- for the children themselves. A collection of their greatest and most exciting moments so they can look back, reflect and talk about their learning both at school and at home.

We suggest that you always include sections on the child's well-being and involvement, as well as their emotional development with clear and detailed references to their interests, their friendships and relationships with adults and peers. Make what you record 'feel like' the child as you know them.

This chapter cannot ignore the current influences on assessment in the Early Years in England. The assessment tool at the time of the Curriculum Guidance for the Foundation Stage (2002) was firmly based on observational assessment. However it was not until a single framework for The Early Years Foundation Stage 0–5 became statutory in 2008 that observational assessment came to the forefront. Teachers became skilled in using the principles of the EYFS to make meaningful observations which could be evaluated and used to inform future considerations for planning and assessment. During this period observations in Reception classes were made in abundance and many practitioners were spending time away from the children on record keeping. The Tickell Review (2010) took note of the invited comments from teachers and other practitioners across the country. It advised that paperwork was excessive and record keeping should be rationalised, so as not to take teachers away from their most important role of interacting with the children. The revised framework (2012) accepted most of the recommendations and as a result there is now statutory guidance. It indicates that assessment should not entail prolonged breaks from interaction with children, nor require excessive paperwork. It strengthens the role of the parent or carer generally, and in particular in the assessment process. You are charged with keeping parents informed of their children's progress and involving them in the process. In real terms this means that assessment must be manageable and is not judged by the amount of physical evidence that is collected but by its accuracy and relevance. 'The impact of observational assessment is not measurable by its weight. It is the use to which the practitioners put their observations that is important' (DfES, 2007, p.8).

Recording learning

Why do we need to record each child's learning development? For many of the same reasons that we record their physical development, medical needs and emotional growth. Records kept by educational and care establishments should have consistency of purpose and be clear, to ensure they are accurately understood. One of the main purposes of record keeping is to monitor progress. This makes it possible to recognise anything that might indicate some difficulty or delay in a child's development. It will also provide evidence for early intervention.

One way to reflect on the importance of observation, assessment and record keeping is to look back at how your parents kept a record of what you did as a child or how you keep a record of your own children over the years. Taking photos, videos, keeping drawings, stories and poems, models and other wonderful constructions to share with family members are all common among families. These can then be enjoyed, looking back to our childhood selves or our own children in earlier years.

A record of learning will help leaders and managers determine the effectiveness of their provision, help the government inspectorate (Ofsted) understand the nature and progress of each child's learning development, and most importantly of all, help parents and children to enjoy together their developing skills and achievements.

Point to ponder

In this current educational climate where record keeping often overtakes worthwhile assessments, there are many challenges presented within everyday practice. Here are just a few to ponder and, in light of this chapter, perhaps be able to find effective solutions. Use the points below as discussion starters with your team.

My time is spent on adult-directed tasks, it is my TA who works alongside the children. How am I able to make worthwhile assessments?

I have to produce x amount of observations a week and only have 2 afternoons to do these observations. How can I do that?

Children only access the outside at playtimes so I have limited opportunity to observe them. How can I assess their learning in this important environment?

Conclusion

We have only begun to touch the surface of this intriguing aspect of our practice. Although it is an aspect that is often viewed disparagingly, we must learn to see it as exciting and invaluable. We hope you have gained insights from our thoughts in this chapter. We hope that they will support and inspire you in developing your contribution to each vital stage of the child's learning. Assessment is complex but it cannot stand alone as a process. It is integral to learning and teaching. In child-initiated experiences and with an enabling environment children are most likely to demonstrate their knowledge, skills and understanding. We have reminded you of the importance of involving parents in their children's learning to create an accurate picture of the child and help move their learning forward. You can read more about this in Chapter 8. We urge you to make your decisions through what feels 'right' to you in providing the best for each child's learning. This is not always easy and will take determination and sometimes courage to achieve. We leave you with this final thought for reflection:

> *'Assessment is a process which must enrich their {children's} lives, their learning and development. Assessment must work for children'.*

> (Drummond 2003, p.13)

Further inspiration

'A Place to Play' by Elizabeth Jarman is an inspiring publication that will help Reception teachers to set up such an environment to meet the needs of both individual and groups of children. Look at the associated website – www.elizabethjarmantraining.co.uk for lots of interesting articles and ideas. If you have not already done so, sign up for her newsletters.

Learning Stories – To find out more about learning stories go to http://tomdrummond. squarespace.com/learning-stories

Making Learning Visible – to find out more read the journal Documentation Panel: The "Making Learning Visible" Project http://www.tandfonline.com/doi/ pdf/10.1080/10901020701878685

Documentation Panels on Pinterest: https://uk.pinterest.com/sarahjwhite/documentation-panels

To find out more about some of the key pioneers go to: http://www.nurseryworld.co.uk/early-years-pioneers

References

Athey, C. (1990) *Extending thought in young children: A parent-teacher partnership.* London: SAGE.

Carr, M. (1998) *Assessing children's learning in early childhood settings: A professional development programme for discussion and reflection.* Wellington: New Zealand Council for Educational Research.

Carr, M. (2001) *Assessment in early years settings: Learning stories.* London: Hodder.

Carr, M. (2004) *Assessment in early childhood education: keeping it complex, keeping it connected, keeping it credible:* a series of three papers based on keynote addresses presented at Te Tari Puna Ora o Aotearoa/NZ Childcare Association national conferences (2001, 2002, 2004). Wellington, New Zealand: Te Tari Puni Ora o Aotearoa/ New Zealand Childcare Association.

Carter, C. and Nutbrown, C. (2010) The tools of assessment: Watching and learning, in G. Pugh and D. Duffy (Eds) *Contemporary issues in the Early Years.* London: Sage.

Clarke, S. (2001) *Unlocking formative asssessment.* London: Hodder.

Department of Education and Skills (DfES) (2007) *Creating the picture.* London: DfES.

Department for Education (DfE) (2012) *Early Years Foundation Stage Revised Framework Statutory Guidance.* London: DfE.

Drummond, M.J. (2003) *Assessing children's learning (2nd ed.).* London: Fulton.

Dubiel, J. (2014) *Effective assessment in the Early Years Foundation Stage.* Early Excellence: London.

Early Education (2012) *Development matters in the Early Years Foundation Stage.* London: Early Education.

Isaacs, S. (1926) *The nursery years.* London: Routledge and Kegan Paul.

Laevers, F. (2006) http://www.kindengezin.be/img/sics-ziko-manual.pdf

Munsch, R. and Martchenko, M. (1980) *The paper bag princess.* New York: Annick Press.

Murphy, J. (2007) *Whatever next.* London: Macmillan.

Nutbrown, C. (2006) *Threads of thinking.* London: SAGE.

Tickell, C. (2010) *The Early Years: Foundations for life, health and learning.* Available at: https://www.gov.uk/government/uploads/system/uploads/attachment_data/file/180919/DFE-00177-2011.pdf

Wien, C. (1997). A Canadian in Reggio Emilia: The May 1997 study tour. *Canadian Children*, 22 (2): 30–8.

Inspirational reading

Arnold, C. (2005) *Observing Harry: Child development and learning, 0–5.* Maidenhead: Open University Press.

Gussin Paley, V. (1990) *The boy who would be a helicopter.* Boston, MA: Harvard University Press.

Marsden, l. and Woodbridge, J. (2005) *Looking closely at learning and teaching.* London: Early Excellence.

Moylett, H. (2011) *Characteristics of effective early learning.* London: Early Education.

Wien, V. (2011) http://ecrp.uiuc.edu/v13n2/wien.html

Jottings

8 You as a partner in the lives of children, families and communities

Gillian Sykes

In this chapter we will begin to consider:

- the many partnerships that Reception teachers make in an effort to support each unique child;
- developing the engagement of parents, families, carers or legal guardians;
- the importance of team working in supporting transitions and enabling a 'community of learning';
- the benefits to multi-professional working;
- the potential of 'community' links;
- the development of creative partnerships.

Introduction

As a Reception teacher we continually strive to safeguard the young children we work with to ensure that all children are able to make good progress. This means that all children should feel included and able to access the curriculum in their own way and at their own level. As discussed in Chapter 2 the Reception teacher can often feel quite isolated, and meeting all children's needs and preferences can seem a mammoth task. However, if we see ourselves as just one link in a complex, yet exciting, community who are interested and care for young children's development, then the task need not seem so daunting. In Chapter 4 Claire talks of the value of the key person role and making secure attachments to ensure that all children feel special and cherished by someone other than a member of their family. Here we begin to ensure that all children feel included, safe, and able to access all aspects of the curriculum.

Yet to do this important role we need to work in partnership with a range of different people and agencies. If we refer back to Bronfenbrenner's ecological framework (1979) (see Chapter 1) and this time by placing the child in the centre, we are able to identify the different systems we should engage with to help the child feel included, respected and valued. By connecting and working with the different groups of people who are important to each individual child's life, we are able to personalise learning and tailor the provision to meet their needs.

This element of our work is multi-faceted. On one hand it can be exciting as we learn new skills, knowledge and understanding from families, colleagues and other professionals. Yet on the other hand it can become rife with difficulties as we try to overcome barriers which may hinder us in making these relationships. Challenges may come in the shape of policy or legislation, or a mismatch of personalities, even time and resources can affect our ability to connect with others. However, if we maintain a positive disposition and a steadfast determination to overcome these barriers we will in the end reap the rewards of partnership working as our children grow and develop as strong, resilient young people.

I liken this to the role of the pedagogista in the schools of Reggio Emilia in Northern Italy. Cagliari et al. (cited in Edwards et al., 2012, p.136) describes the pedagogista (co-ordinator) 'as embedded in a system of relationships with other teachers, other school staff, parents, citizens, administrators, public officials and outside audiences. The pedagogista cannot interact with just one part of the system and leave the rest aside, because that would injure the whole'. There is no expectation that we could or should seek to replicate this practice, but instead learn from it and respond to what we have learnt to benefit our own community of learners.

Therefore this chapter will consider the different partnerships we should develop in an effort to provide a rich, appropriate curriculum for all children. It will begin by discussing the most important of partnerships, that of parents and families. This will be followed by the vital aspect of team work, firstly within the Reception class and then within the community of the school. This section will also consider the crucial collaboration of pre-school practitioners and how successful transitions need to be planned for, and developed. If we are ensuring we place the child at the centre of our work we must, at times, also solicit the help of other professionals. These other professionals may be from other agencies, within the child's local community or indeed from other 'creative' partnerships.

In essence, we need a 'shared image of the child'.

Team talks and tasks

As a team begin to note the different partnerships you should develop. Think about each of the children in your group and identify the different ecological systems that may influence their learning and development.

Engaging with parents and families

The title of this sub-section has been carefully considered. Building a positive relationship requires mutual understanding and respect, and an underlying desire to make things work. Therefore parents and families need to understand why this partnership is so important. There needs to be opportunities to inform them about their children's learning and occasions where they can be involved. In other words, there needs to be a 'willing engagement'. You will also note that the term families has been included in this section. In today's society, children are not necessarily cared for by their birth parents, and while we talk of parents we also need to think in the wider terms of primary carer, legal guardian and wider family.

The thought of engaging with parents and families is one which may fill many Reception teachers, young and old, with dread. Yet, the benefits of working with parents far outweigh any reservations we may have, and therefore lack of confidence in developing these partnerships is not an option. As a Reception teacher, from the first meetings with parents I would set out to win their trust and 'friendship'. Many people would argue against teachers making friends with parents. However, the 'friendship' I am suggesting here has professional boundaries that value the traits of:

- mutual respect – *I respect you as a parent, you respect me as a teacher;*

- a common bond – *their child or children (remember you may teach more than one sibling);*

- a common interest – *the well-being and development of their child;*

- trust – *parents need to trust that you know what you are doing and that you have the best interests of their child at heart;*

- an attachment to each other – *not just important to children but also to adults (is there someone at school that I can go to if I am worried about my child?);*

- good will – *where kindness is reciprocated;*

- emotional safety – *parents need to feel comfortable in your company and happy to talk about their child;*

- is rarely one-sided – *you need to do everything in your power to develop your relationship with all families;*

- culturally diverse – *remember friendship means different things to different people, so we need to tread carefully.*

Remember that the care and education of each precious child is in your hands. This is quite a responsibility and therefore you need all the help you can get. The Early Years Foundation Stage (2007) states quite clearly that 'Parents are children's first and most enduring educators'. They know about their foibles and quirks. They understand what makes them tick and can provide an insight into their behaviour at home and with family and friends. It is these intricacies that we need to know about to enable us to nurture a child's learning and development. Therefore, an effective partnership needs to be established from the outset. Curtis and O'Hagan (2009, p.100) ask us to remember these six *positive* things when seeking to engage with parents:

1. All families have strengths.

2. Parents can learn new techniques.

3. Parents have important perspectives about their children.

4. Most parents really care about their children.

5. Cultural differences are both valid and valuable.

6. Many family forms exist and are legitimate.

If we unpick each of these six points we will begin to get a clearer picture of our role in developing this partnership.

1. All families have strengths

This first point is especially important as often we do not value the families we have. Strengths come in many different guises. The strengths may lie in the skills they have, for example: an uncle who can play an instrument to inspire children, or a mum who is a dentist who can teach the children about how to look after their teeth, or a granny who can knit resources, or a dad who is a chef and who can come in to cook with the children. It may be the opportunities they can provide, for example: fitting an outdoor tap, organising a gardening weekend, locating resources for particular themes, or bringing in a bird of prey. Sometimes it may be the simplest of things that make the biggest impact, for example: it may be the patience they can provide, the playfulness they can demonstrate, or the stories they can tell. Often parents don't recognise the strengths they have, or have the confidence to offer their help. Because of this it is up to us to validate their efforts and to show gratitude for their help. The examples above are all real life examples of which I have many, many more. The key to success is having the 'will' to find out about the families you work with and then drawing upon this source of experience, energy and expertise.

Point to ponder

How might you find out about your parents' and families' strengths? Which parents do you call upon to help? Are there any parents who meld into the background?

2. Parents can learn new techniques

If we want parents to be able to support their children then we need them to understand what we are doing and why. Here the most important aspect is the 'why'. This will help parents to understand about child development, and how children learn. In Chapter 2 Eleonora has provided comprehensive, carefully considered theory on child development to help you provide a clear rationale to parents. There are a raft of ideas to inform and involve parents, yet once again we need to reflect on these from the parents' perspective. In one class of children we will have a social mix of parents, all having had their own experiences of 'schooling' and all having very different feelings regarding education. Therefore, it is essential that we enable all parents to be able to access the opportunity to 'learn new techniques'. Just as with children, we need to think about your parents' and families' unique needs and preferences. By providing a range of options you should be able to tailor this involvement to ensure inclusion for even the hardest to reach families. You will have your own creative ideas for this, and technology is making this increasingly simple. You might email links to, for example, Pinterest, blogs or interesting reports that can stimulate and inform parents. There is no guarantee that parents will access these, but by offering these opportunities you are saying 'we are partners in supporting your child's development'. You should have a policy which clearly states that parents are expected to be fully involved in their children's learning. Parents need to be invited in to the classroom in the morning to drop their children off. Then if 'learning is made visible', as if by osmosis parents will begin to understand what constitutes effective Early Years practice. For those parents who are unable to drop their children off through work commitments, you need to consider other means of gaining knowledge and a joint understanding. Suggestions could include holding 'celebration events' (where the children share their learning), workshops which involve the parents and children, open afternoons or trips away from school on neutral ground.

Vignette

I had a particularly hard to reach group of parents who did not feel comfortable coming into school. After numerous attempts and little uptake I went out into the playground at the end of the day and asked for their advice. I gave some suggestions and then asked some of the least receptive parents to gather some feedback. By elevating their positions and giving them responsibility for procuring the information I quickly received positive feedback. They did the organisation of the events and I did the informal 'what we are doing and why' input. Photographs and videos of their children helped them to understand what this learning looked like in practice. We had for example: fish and chip suppers, picnics at the park, and bingo evenings. This growing friendship meant that they then felt able to come into school for informal workshops with their children.

3. Parents have important perspectives about their children

The key to this point is that we show that we *really* value parents' knowledge of their child. This needs to be authentic, as parents can quickly recognise when we are not truly listening to them. Therefore, Hughes and Read (2012, p.27) would urge us to listen with our ears, eyes, mind and heart. They highlight seven qualities of a good listener, which will help you to demonstrate your interest in learning about parents' perspectives:

1. Empathy, attunement and presence

2. Warmth

3. Respect for others

4. Genuineness

5. Sense of humour

6. Sense of humility

7. Self-awareness.

Team talks and tasks

As noted earlier we know that parents are a key source to understanding about the uniqueness of their child. Therefore, discuss each of these points in your team so that you can fully understand how you can tune into what parents are sharing with you. Consider introducing peer observations to look at interactions with parents.

4.   Most parents really care about their children

I have often argued that *all* parents 'love' their children and want what is best for them. But I also state that love can look very different, and need not necessarily manifest itself as we would expect it to. I recognise this is an idealist notion and therefore Hughes and Read's use of the word 'most' instead of 'all' might be a better choice. Hence 'most' parents will have aspirations for their children and will want to ensure that they are in the care of people who also 'love' their children. Here again I am keen to ruffle a few feathers. Love is often regarded as a taboo word. However, if we truly love the children we are working with the children can feel safe, and parents can sleep well in the knowledge that their child's well-being is being nurtured. Chapter 7 looks at how we can involve and inform parents in the assessment of their children's learning.

5.   Cultural differences are both valid and valuable

Cultural diversity is exciting as well as challenging. We do live in a multicultural society and should therefore embrace and celebrate the unique perspectives of our community of children and families. By talking openly to families we can begin to understand about beliefs, traditions and cultures and enable children and their families to respect and value one another. At a time of growing concern over radicalisation we need to do everything we can to be sensitive yet resolute in our determination to treat people with respect and equality. Likewise, you may have a growing number of refugee and asylum seeker families who may be traumatised, vulnerable and possibly distrusting. Your classroom may provide a safe haven for these families. Central to developing these relationships is an awareness that different cultures have different styles of communication, belief and values. At all times we should treat others sensitively and remain professional and sincere. But most importantly be yourself.

?

Point to ponder

When you share a story with a parent and child you are creating a triangle of love and trust. This triangle forms the links and interactions between each group. The Reggio Emilia Approach refer to this as 'The triangle of relationships' (Thornton and Brunton, 2007, p.12) which sits within its own cultural and social environment. Is this evident in your practice?

---

6.   Many family forms exist and are legitimate

The final point that Curtis and O'Hagan raise is the acknowledgement that many family forms exist and are legitimate. Our society is made up of different family structures and no two families are the same. We should, at all times, remain unbiased in our views and not pass judgement. Instead, we should be open and accepting and ensure that children have a sense of worth and a positive identity.

Point to ponder

How do you avoid letting your inner feelings and attitudes affect your work with parents and families? How do you remain unbiased?

The EYFS (DfES, 2007) states that 'when parents and practitioners work together in early years settings, the results have a positive impact on children's development and learning'. Curtis and O'Hagan (2009, p.100) maintain that when forming relationships with parents the set of skills required include 'good listening techniques, tact, kindness, consideration, empathy, enthusiasm and an understanding of parent-child relationships'. This section has only touched the surface of this important partnership, but most of the chapters in this book refer to and confirm its significance in providing effective provision.

Team talks and tasks

The Reggio Emilia Schools of Northern Italy believe that 'parents are entitled to help shape the future educational experience of their children' (Thornton and Brunton, 2009, p.128).

Discuss. Do you hold this belief? Do the contributions from parents influence what you do? How do you show that the ideas and views of parents are worthy of consideration and discussion? Re-examine how you engage with families.

Team working

The importance of working as a team cannot be disputed as it supports a collegiate approach to your work with young children and their parents. At no time should the Reception teacher feel alone, and in fact it should be your role to build a team around you where you can discuss ideas, evaluate learning, exchange information and share responsibility. Working collaboratively and cooperatively provides the foundations for developing and enhancing provision.

An image of children and childhood should be agreed up on, as this will then be reflected in your policies and practices. Mutual understanding is paramount as it helps provide a united front and a consistency of messages. Strong underpinning beliefs in a system of democracy also places a recognition and value on capitalising on individuals' knowledge and skills. The size of a team can vary greatly and in some schools could be just two people. This then requires a relationship that is based on respect, honesty and patience, a little like a marriage. Conversely a team may be made of three classes and ten adults. In this instance, careful planning of time to work together is critical. Either case calls for a team dedicated to playing their part in providing top quality provision. As children are great observers it should follow that if they see practitioners working together happily and enthusiastically they then mirror these behaviours.

Reflective and reflexive practice is essential to keep provision current and dynamic. However, to be critically reflective calls for a team culture where all contributions are valued and respected, irrespective of status. High levels of mutual trust and respect provide a safe platform on which different perspectives can be shared and discussed. Ann Whitehouse (in Hayes et al., 2014, p. 51) suggests that the impact of confident critically reflective practitioners 'spreads far, like a ripple, reaching children, parents, colleagues, peers, organisations, communities and the wider society'. This synergy and stimulation is illustrated beautifully in Claire's chapter on collaboration and the impact of the Miró Project (see Chapter 5).

However, it is equally vital that we extend our community of learning to those who work with our youngest children (pre-school provision) and those who work with our older children (Key Stages 1 and 2). Without this collaborative working a smooth continuum of development cannot be achieved. Samantha in Chapter 3 skilfully writes about the importance of being an advocate for Early Childhood Education and Care and likens us to 'one of the cogs that is turning the movement of education as a whole'. Yet for this to happen we need to be proactive in raising the profile of the Early Years. Our voices need to be united and strong. Imagine your team throwing large handfuls of pebbles into the sea and the ripples, splashes and waves this could create. In the same way if we work:

- collegiately – we need to be able to justify what we are saying;

- collaboratively – as there is strength in numbers;

- determinedly – we need to be unwavering in our quest;

- consideredly – 'what do I want this community of people to know?';

- sensitively – an awareness and respect of your audience.

then we can influence what our colleagues know of Early Years education. In working in this way, we help to shape the educational experience for all children.

It is pleasing to note that in recent years there has been a real shift in thinking regarding the important links necessary between pre-school provision and schools. With the gradual increase of graduates coming in to Early Years settings, provision has continued to improve and with this a commitment to improving the transitions for young children. By making this process a continual one, children, parents and practitioners are reaping the benefits. In a similar vein, closer working with primary colleagues, in different projects, supports them in getting to know the children who will in time become their pupils. Additionally it helps us to 'showcase' what effective Early Years teaching and learning looks like. Peer observations are an excellent means of sharing good practice and elevating the work we do in the Reception year. It also helps you to raise your professional identity as your colleagues witness your children enthusiastically and independently engaged in deep learning. How often have we heard, 'Oh now I understand. I had thought they were just playing'?

Team talks and tasks

Assign your class the responsibility of creating a 'welcome book' for children coming from pre-school to school. Let them take photographs of their favourite places and let them write about the things they enjoy doing at school. When new children visit they can become the tour leaders. Evaluate the effectiveness of this. Suggest similar ideas to other classes within school.

Multi-agency working

In England, *Working Together to Safeguard Children* (DfE, 2015) was published, by the government, to provide statutory guidance on inter-agency working to safeguard and promote the welfare of children. This is a child-centred and coordinated approach to safeguarding and identifying children and families who would benefit from early help. Over the years difficulties have arisen as specialists within single agency contexts have found it difficult to move to work as part of a multi-professional team. Anning et al. (2006, p.162) found that when 'differences in beliefs, values, and approaches … were acknowledged, confronted and reconciled teams were able to move forward more effectively'. With the introduction of 'Working Together to Safeguard Children' this has further supported different teams working together. By working with others, we are becoming more adept at recognising signs which could be putting children at risk or where early intervention is needed. A Reception teacher holds key information about the children they work with, is tuned into their behaviours, has in-depth observations and good relationships with parents. Therefore we must feel confident in our professional competence and take steps when worried to identify and share concerns. Be clear about safeguarding procedures and recognise that we are just one part of the 'team around the child'.

Trodd (2011, p.45) recognises the problems arising as people attempt to define which profession, professional or professionalism fits with current Early Years working. Whether we are working with, for example, Speech and Language Therapists, Educational Psychologists, Health Visitors or Social Workers, Oberhuemer (2005, p.13) proposes that we are all 'democratic professionals'. She states that democratic professionals 'open up opportunities for debate, encourages others to ask questions rather than accept received traditions of thought and encourages critical thinking in their area of work'. However, I rather like Rinaldi's (2005, p.126) description of a 'dialogic professional'. I think we have a lot to learn from this construct, which draws on 'social interaction and active participation in learning and thinking'. She pinpoints 'active listening, responsiveness to others and respect for their autonomy as key qualities of professional behaviour and essential features of professionalism' (2005, p.126). This view of a 'dialogic professional' presents an image of someone who is kind, honest and open to change and uncertainty. A dialogic professional, or indeed a 'democratic professional' is open to others' views and opinions and is therefore more able to work in partnership with others. They do not see threats to professional identity, but instead want to learn from others in the best interest of the child.

Indeed, interagency working and opportunities for training from, and with, other professionals means:

- knowledge is shared and broadened;

- there is a positivity for different roles;

- communication is strengthened;

- there is a greater confidence in understanding;

- an awareness of where to go for extra support;

- an insight into the complexities of different roles;

- an awareness of issues other professionals might face;

- a greater professionalism and respect.

Consider here the parallels we can draw to our work with families and our team.

Point to ponder

Would you describe yourself as a 'dialogic or a democratic professional'? How many different agencies do you work with to support the children and families in your class?

One of the joys of being deemed an effective Reception teacher means that your local Early Years SEN Inclusion Team will recommend you to families with children with specific needs. This is a real privilege and means that you will work with children with a range of 'special rights'. This concept of 'special rights' is one coined by the Reggio Approach and sits well in a curriculum rooted in the United Nations Convention of the Rights of the Child (1989). With this privilege comes a huge responsibility to ensure that you are meeting the diverse needs of all children. However, if we look at this with a positive lens we recognise the potential for professional development and learning.

Vignette

Many years ago we were asked to accept a little boy with cerebral palsy. We were told that he could not walk, or talk and was not toilet trained. However, his parents, and grandparents, were keen for him to be in a mainstream school. Although anxious, we were keen to support the family and we began do our own research into cerebral palsy. Working in a small mobile classroom we considered the challenges that this little boy might face. Meeting with his parents we were struck by their positivity and determination and I agreed to go and meet him in one of his 'conductive education sessions'. His grandma, who explained in more detail about Conductive Education, accompanied me. Entering the building, I was struck by the optimism that filled the room. Families, children and practitioners engaged in all types of activities to help them in improving their motor skills and movements. It was there I met this little boy with a smile that reached from ear to ear. Working with a range of professionals, we began to develop our knowledge and understanding to enable us to support his development. This little boy soon turned out to be a source of inspiration to all who met him and worked with him. His sheer dogged determination often put us to shame, as we watched him take his first steps and say his first few laboured words. How we loved that little boy. He is now a young man who has been to college and is earning a living working with, and caring for animals. I sometimes see him walking through town with his friends and feel honoured to have learnt so much through him and with him.

I have many similar stories, but without being a 'dialogic professional', open minded and empathetic, maybe I would never have had the courage and opportunity to develop through and with others.

Community partnerships

The concept of relationships and partnerships is one which extends far beyond that of the more recognised ones of parents and families, and incorporates the wider communities in which the children live and interact. If we view children as young citizens then their education should be extended to the environments they occupy as part of their community. By capitalising on the opportunities the community can provide the children will begin to learn about citizenship and democracy. As described in Chapter 6, by taking children into shared public or social spaces they learn to respect and value the different people they meet. By providing positive learning experiences within their local neighbourhood, children will develop a sense of belonging and a positive identity.

There has been much in the media about the decline of communities and the importance of the improvement and regeneration of neighbourhoods. We know that children's life chances are affected by the community in which they grow up (Marmot, 2010). Areas of deprivation have an impact upon children's health, well-being and their potential for educational achievement. How then, as a Reception teacher, can we address the many inequalities children face?

> ### ? Point to ponder
>
> What are the demographics for your area? What are the implications for the children and families living in this area? How can you find out about community renewal schemes?

As emphasised throughout this book it is key to actively involve children in planning their own learning. Added to this 'mixing pot' of expectations comes their understanding of the relevance of being a responsible citizen. We should not underestimate children's ability and eagerness to connect with 'real life' situations. Children, just like adults, like to feel a sense of worth and respond positively when charged with a 'purpose' or 'goal'. If these then relate to community-based projects then learning is twofold. Children learn how to be responsible and caring, and the community learn about the value of truly listening and engaging with young children. Once again I draw from the practice of Reggio Emilia where it is seen as the responsibility of the schools to give back to the community and to respond to the changes in society. Giacopini (2000) describes this relationship and states:

> *Education should occupy public spaces and not solely be within the walls of the institution. Reggio schools are set within the city and visible to the city. The city of the children, the city for the children.*

For us we need to interchange the word *city* to *community*:

'The community of the children, the community for the children'.

Now we can begin to think about our role as a Reception teacher in developing this philosophy and transforming it into a reality.

Vignette

This example is one inspired by a project I jointly led on the work of the artist Joan Miró. A small group of teachers and practitioners used the work of Miró as an inspirational starting point for children's learning. The work evolved following the children's ideas and preferences.

Figures 8.1a-c Artwork arising from 'Project Miró' by children at Sheringham Primary School

(Continued)

(Continued)

Keen to share the children's creations, the teachers organised exhibitions where the children invited family, friends and the local community in for private viewings. Many also invited local dignitaries and governors to celebrate the children's successes, and their work was featured in the local tabloids. One small village school invited the 'senior citizens' art group' for a cup of tea and a personal tour of the exhibition. This resulted in them forming a wonderful partnership. The children then took their portfolios of art and displayed their work in the local retirement home and library.

Many schools are now involved in creating posters, designed by the children, which are displayed around their local communities reminding people to take their litter home.

Another example of what McDowall Clark (2013, p.117) calls 'meaningful participation' is when we were involved in creating a 'multi-sensory' garden at the local church. Working closely with a local business and the parish council, the children gave their views and ideas, through drawings and photographs. A design was drawn up and then the children and their families, with a little 'muscle' provided by some university students, created a garden which could be enjoyed by all.

These are large-scale projects which take effort and commitment. Yet we know that these types of projects have a lasting 'effect' on the children and their families, as they are strengthened by the emotions they arouse and the memories they leave. Again, this demonstrates the importance of the Reception teacher's role in forging these diverse partnerships.

Team talks and tasks

Consider a 'big project' which could involve your local community. Make sure you document your project and then share this with your local school Early Years network.

Creative partnerships

The final section of this chapter seeks to ignite a spark in all new, old and trainee Reception teachers, to pursue new and creative partnerships: partnerships which will help in bringing the arts, culture and creative approaches into the lives of children. In 1999 The National Advisory Committee on Creative and Cultural Education (NACCCE) produced the report, *All Our Futures: Creativity, Culture and Education*. This was led by Sir Ken Robinson who called for the promotion of the creative development of children and the encouragement of an ethos which supports and values cultural diversity. It argued 'that creativity will be increasingly important to businesses and the economy in the next century and that the school curriculum will need to reflect this'. This report resulted in many schools developing 'creative curriculums'. And for many it confirmed what we already knew and were doing, but opened up other doors. It became a blueprint for an education system relevant and meaningful for young people in the twenty-first century. The government at this time were keen to develop these partnerships and money was provided to foster and support schools and organisations to work together. Although there has since been changes in government, most arts and cultural organisations have educational experts keen to develop links with schools. It is yet another of our roles to seek out and develop these relationships.

For many children the world of culture and the arts may appear to be something they might only encounter second hand. Indeed, for many families a trip to a museum or art gallery may not feature in their lives. However, if we recognise the importance of creativity on humans' capacity to develop new ideas or to have original thought (Craft, 2002), then we need to provide experiences which may nourish this. This goes beyond the 'creativity' associated with classroom teaching, and into the realms of new experiences, which can ignite and enthuse. Experiences which open new doors to new worlds. Children need to be able to immerse themselves in dance or art and to be transported into an imaginary world by, for example, a professional storyteller or a trip to the theatre.

Often we put risk assessments and logistics as barriers to accessing these opportunities. But as discussed in Chapter 6, we should be thinking in terms of 'risk benefits'. Logistics can generally be overcome if you weigh up the long-term advantages of each new experience to the children you are working with.

Vignette

Working in partnership with an artist is something which is often difficult to organise. However, our local art college has many students who are keen to develop works of art through working with young children. One particular student wanted to develop a nursery rhyme trail in our local community. Working with small groups of children she developed their ideas to create bronze tiles which she embedded into the footpaths around the children's local community. The children were involved in each of the stages and were then keen to take family and friends on their nursery rhyme trail. The pleasure of finding their own tile was a joy to behold.

We were also lucky to be able to take our children to the theatre to see an immersive theatre production of 'The Wind in the Willows'. Keen to involve the parents and families we ensured every child had someone special to them to accompany them. There was a cost involved in this, but we ran a fund raising event to help subsidise the payments. For many of you 'pupil premium' can be used creatively to support the children's development. The delight shown on the adults' faces, as well as the children's, was proof enough that the effort in organising the trip had far outweighed the difficulties.

If the cost is too high, many theatre or dance companies will come into school to perform. So be innovative in your thinking. Many cultural centres have free entry, and the educationalists there will provide rich experiences to generate learning. Remember all children should have access to these experiences. By developing these partnerships, Reception teachers learn new skills and knowledge to use with children in the future.

Figure 8.2 The joy of finding a nursery rhyme tile

Conclusion

If we visualise each child standing centre stage, we can begin to identify the different partners we need to work with to support that child in performing to the best of their ability. Each child will have different people who interact in their lives who can hinder or support their functioning. As a Reception teacher we are just one of these links in a huge network. It is just one of our roles to facilitate the team around the child.

Further inspiration

View the eBook produced following the Miró Project entitled: Project Miró: An international and multi-sited journey of Early Years creative practice, inspired by the artist Joan Miró on:https://itunes.apple.com/gb/book/project-miro/id887943037?mt=11

Be inspired by the stunning ebook 'Beauty, Miró, Children,' http://www.albelli.co.uk/view-online-photo-book/d382057b-bf38-4dc6-ad65-c3c4bfddd5e9

Visit, for example, your local theatre, art gallery, museum, etc. and speak to their educationalist

Watch the Ted Talk 'Do Schools kill Creativity' by Sir Ken Robinson https://www.youtube.com/watch?v=iG9CE55wbtY

References

Anning, A. (2006) 'Setting the national scene', in Anning, A. and Edwards, A. *Promoting children's learning from birth to five: Developing the new early years professional, 2nd ed.* Maidenhead: Open University Press.

Bronfenbrenner, U. (1979) *The ecology of human development.*Cambridge, MA: Harvard University Press.

Craft, A. (2002) *Creativity and early years education.* London: Continuum.

Curtis, A. and O'Hagan, M. (2009) *Care and education in early childhood: A students guide to theory and practice (2nd ed.).* Abingdon: Routledge.

DfE (2015) *Working together to safeguard children.* Available online at: www.gov.uk/government/publications Reference: DFE-00130-2015 (accessed 3 March 2016)

DfES (2007) *The Early Years Foundation Stage.* Nottingham: DfES Publications.

Giacopini, E. (2000) in Thornton, L. and Brunton, P. (2009) *Understanding the Reggio Approach: Early years education in practice* (2nd ed.). Abingdon: Routledge.

Hayes, C., Daly, J., Duncan, M., Gill, R. and Whitehouse, A. (2014) *Developing as a reflective early years professional: A thematic approach.* Northwich: Critical Publishing.

Hughes, A. and Read, V. (2012) *Building positive relationships with parents and young children: A guide to effective communication.* Abingdon: Routledge.

McDowall Clark, R. (2013) *Childhood in society for the early years* (2nd ed.). London: SAGE.

Marmot, M. (2010) *Fair society, healthy lives: The Marmot Review.* London.

Oberhuemer, P. (2005) Conceptualising the early childhood pedagogue: policy approaches ad issues of professionalism. *European Early Childhood Research Journal,* 7 (1):5–16.

Rinaldi, C. (2005) *In dialogue with Reggio Emilia.* London: Routledge.

Thornton, L. and Brunton, P. (2007) *Bringing the Reggio Approach to your early years practice.* Abingdon: Routledge.

Thornton, L. and Brunton, P. (2009) *Understanding the Reggio Approach: Early years education in practice* (2nd ed.). Abingdon: Routledge.

Trodd, L. and Chivers, L. (Eds) (2011) *Interprofessional working in practice: Learning and working together for children and families.* Maidenhead: McGrawHill.

Jottings

9 You in a team of researchers

Anna Cox

In this chapter we will begin to consider:

- learning as a research activity;
- the classroom as a research community;
- the impact of the classroom climate on young learner researchers;
- the potential of systematic research to understand and develop practice;
- the role of practitioner research;
- using research done by others to develop your practice.

Introduction

In the Reception year children are encouraged to be researchers, supported by the provision made available to them by you, their teacher. You do this informed by what you know about them and informed by what is known about how young children learn. Young learners can be seen as individual researchers attending to their areas of interest. However, alongside this they work as a team or community, sharing knowledge from their research to create a climate in which new ideas are shared and cognitive development flourishes. As a Reception teacher you are both the facilitator of this research team and a member of it, a fellow researcher. You bring to fruition children's individual research and are ideally placed to do your own research too. In this chapter we consider teaching and learning in the Reception classroom as a research community and the teacher's role in enabling this. We will consider how the emotional climate of the classroom influences children's capacity to take risks and experiment in their learning and we will consider the role of the teacher as a researcher, which is a long valued but not always clearly understood feature of professional practice. Finally, we will look at the importance of other research in supporting our practice and how this can be accessed and employed as part of continuing professional development.

In Chapter 7, Shona and Julia discussed the role of observation and its value in understanding children's learning. Observation has also been used more formally as a research tool and one of the early projects to do this was the 'Observational Research and Classroom Learning Evaluation' studies (known as ORACLE), which took place in the 1970s. It was reported by Galton, Hargreaves, Comber and Wall in 1980. At that time, many primary teachers were creating enquiry-based learning opportunities for children and these lent themselves well to the use of ICT-supported observations. Recording teachers at work was possible and allowed closer unpicking of lessons than could be done in real time. Despite the apparent focus on enquiry and the use of questions to stimulate children's thinking, Galton found that teacher talk dominated classroom conversations in the 1970s study rather than pupils sharing ideas. Interestingly the work was repeated by the team almost 20 years later (Galton et al., 1999) and teacher talk had increased! This large-scale use of observation as a research tool has something important to say both about the technique and the difference between perceptions and research-informed understandings in the education of young children. It had not been anticipated that teacher talk would have increased in the classroom but it had.

Observation as a research tool is not the same as watching, and focused observation as a research tool can reveal much that we miss in the moment as busy Reception teachers. The use of video recording can be an influential tool in researching our own practice. Some teacher training provision has been giving tablet devices to trainees and getting them to video record parts of lessons and to reflect on them via video too. One provider sharing information about this is the University of Hull. The project is described on the university website www2.hull. ac.uk and can be found by searching 'ipad use by teacher trainees' (last accessed January 2016).

The use of video-based research can be used to capture all of an event and unpick it or perhaps more usefully to look at and reflect on parts of a lesson. This will be considered later in this chapter.

Children's learning as research

Piaget's description of children operating as lone scientists plays well with the notion of learning as research. Children's efforts to understand the world around them become increasingly systematic as they gain and use knowledge, so seeing them as researchers is an unsurprising idea. However, a bit of further unpicking about learning as research is also useful. Enquiry-based learning (EBL), sometimes Inquiry-based learning (IBL) is extensively discussed, valued for the development of thinking skills and for enabling children to generate their own ideas about things that they want to learn more about (Eick and Reed, 2002). It is a common approach in science teaching in particular but lends itself to less subject-specific learning for younger children. They are able to build on their previous knowledge and understanding, develop enquiring minds and are encouraged to make sense of the world for themselves. EBL not only inspires children to learn for themselves, it also brings a research-orientated approach.

A practical and accessible approach to EBL is using PNI. This provides a structure for thinking about problems by recording positive, negative, and interesting ideas about an issue to open discussion and widen thinking. De Bono (1985, 1988) is well known for a number of ways to support and develop thinking skills, one of which is PMI (here the word negative is substituted by minus). It can work well in a Reception classroom full of enquiring minds.

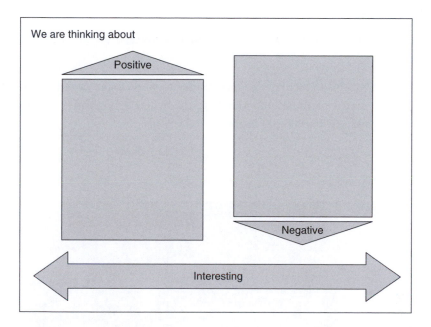

Figure 9.1 An example PNI diagram

This kind of format can be used for whole class sharing of ideas, in small groups or individually. It helps children to be able to start to classify their ideas and then to make some conclusions. It can also help young learners understand that views and ideas other than their own are worthy of consideration. These are useful research skills and useful life skills for children. PNI lends itself well to what Claxton (2002) calls playful or convivial learning, and to what Perkins (1995) calls *wild topics*, or those that genuinely excite and stimulate children. Wild topics are intended to expand children's learning capacity as well as cover what we usually think of as content knowledge. They have to be engaging enough for four-year-old children to want to pursue them! Below is a list of some of the criteria which are likely to make a project or activity be of interest to young learners.

Try to make the topic:

- *deep and rich*, so the children will have lots to find out about;

- *challenging*, so they will need to look at factual books you provide, make observations and ask others;

- *extended*, so that there is time for deep-level learning and opportunities to go into the topic in depth;

- *relevant*, so that it connects with children's own interests and concerns that you have observed;

- *child led,* so that your class have some genuine control over what, why, how and when they organise their learning;

- *unfamiliar or unknown*: the teacher does not already know the 'answer' and you will learn together;

- *collaborative*: many children enjoy the opportunity to work together with others on such tasks but some may contribute individually to the 'whole' (sometimes called working synchronously and asynchronously in the digital world).

Adapted from Claxton (2007, p.126)

Figure 9.2 Collaborating to explore the unknown

Team talks and tasks

With the other adults you work with consider this example for PNI:
Would it be a good thing if plants could walk about? Do you think
that children in your class could identify positive points? How could you help them
to think about negative points? What might be interesting about the idea but not
positive nor negative? How would you work with your class to summarise the
discussion?

Look at your long-term plan. Do you have any 'wild topics' in it? What wild topic
could you put in, in place of something you have used before?

Developing a rich culture of research in your classroom

The development of language is very fully described in Chapter 2, from the perspective of
child development. Here I discuss ways in which children develop vocabulary to support
them as researchers. It is not difficult to justify thinking about children as researchers. In
a special edition of *Early child development and care*, Murray (2013) puts forward the view
that there are behaviours commonly seen (and able to be encouraged in young children)
that count as research behaviour. In particular she suggests that natural problem-solving
behaviours reveal higher order thinking skills. As a Reception teacher you will promote
confidence in the children and seek to empower them, you will thrive on understanding
the perspectives of children in your class and so you are ideally placed to support research
language as well as research behaviour.

Taking away the role of the adult as an arbiter of what is worth finding out more
about is crucial if children are to thrive as researchers. No one who has worked with
children in the Reception year doubts their creativity and this is a valuable research skill.
By thinking of creativity as a research skill the focus is on the teacher to encouraging
divergent thinking and provide children with interesting things to think about.
Solutions to the challenges of the future will not be found by considering
only the ways of the past and so creative thinking among young learners must be valued.
Using questioning skills, providing appropriate resources and allowing time for
children to explore the environment and those wild topics will support their
natural creativity.

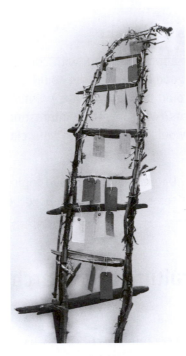

Figure 9.3 An imaginative way to collect children's ideas

Figure 9.4 Children researching together — 'so this is what you can do in mud!'

Your judgement and children's judgement in shared research

For adults not familiar with young children's learning the notion that they exercise judgement might seem unlikely. Those familiar with these active minds are of course aware of children's developing capacity to make judgements. As young researchers they are able to classify and order items in the environment, they assess risk in their play as they explore the physical environment and they make judgements in other contexts too. As a Reception teacher you are uniquely placed to help children gain confidence in their judgements and to think about what information they call on to make them. Strategies include those already talked about, such as the wild topics and the PMI model in the previous section. The use of effective questioning by the teacher is also a key contributor to the research culture of the classroom. Since research is about questions, this is not too surprising. The speed with which children comment on what is fair and not fair can provide an effective base from which to build skills in judgement. 'Why?' and 'what if' are likely to populate the discourse that follows some event seen as unfair. The range of interaction strategies now known as sustained shared thinking (Siraj-Blatchford et al., 2002) and mentioned in Chapter 4 can help Reception teachers on their journey to making the most of their interactions with children. For this kind of interaction to take place the importance of the relationship between the adult and child must be mutually respectful. Helping children to be confident to make judgements sits well within a community that values sustained shared thinking and in which respectful relationships exist.

Research through thought provoking communication and dialogic teaching

Early in the relationship with a class it is not uncommon for children to make interjections on topics which to the teacher seem unrelated to what is going on at that moment. Children's need to share what is happening in their heads can serve the teacher well, helping us to know children better and identify their needs and desires, likes and dislikes and their preferences for some things over others. Purposeful communication develops from these early unconnected sharings, a refinement of them as children's understanding of the nature of dialogue increases. One of a range of ways to increase this effective communication is through the use of 'dialogic teaching'. Alexander (2004) describes dialogic talk as a means to harness the power of talk to stimulate and extend children's thinking and advance their learning and understanding. Dialogic teaching is more than questions and answers and not just any talk. Advocates of the approach say that it is quite different from question and answer and information transmission strategies seen in some classrooms. Alexander highlights the importance of interactions that encourage children to think, and to think in different ways, hence my link to research. He emphasises that questions should invite more from children than just recall; recall is not interesting for the children or for you in most cases. Teachers are encouraged to ask children to justify their answers and to guide children to follow up and build on what they know. He highlights the value of effective feedback to young learners. The feedback that you give to children (individually or in groups) must inform and lead thinking forward as well as providing encouragement to them. Enthusiasm and positivity in dialogue with children cannot be undervalued and it is really good to smile! Giving children thinking time without interruption is becoming increasingly common in Reception classrooms and practical strategies to do this are ideas like 'think, pair, share' or an idea of mine which I call a 'me moment'. A 'me moment' is the think without the pair. It allows children to store up an idea until they can develop it more fully. Holding on to your own good idea seems to excite lots of children, in my experience, as long as you do come back and collect the ideas in a timely way. Some Reception teachers do this through a class question book – where things worth finding out about, or in my terms research, are recorded to be worked on in the future. Such a book should be beautiful drawing children in to finding out about all manner of things. Pictures can enhance the book and the further activities to address the children's questions should be recorded in images and words too.

Other ideas from dialogic teaching are supporting the linking together of ideas and valuing alternative ideas, not just taking everything at face value and you can model this for the children through articulating your own thinking. You can show them that you too want to find things out and be a researcher. Alexander also places high value on secure and professional subject knowledge for teaching. This, he suggests, helps teachers take learning forward beyond 'normal' boundaries set by age-related expectations. Some of the children in your class will amaze you with what they know and understand. How exciting it is to encourage them to be researchers and continue into their extended learning. Alexander does not mention something that is important in my thinking – that children should be aware that there are things the teacher does not know and wants to find out about.

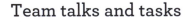

Team talks and tasks

With the other adults you work with, each make an individual list of ten words that describe the climate of your classroom. Share one of the lists and tally how many others used those words. One by one ask people if they have additional words and again tally if others have them. How long is your list? Which are the most popular words among the team? What does this tell you about shared values and ideas that support young researchers?

Collaboration and a community of practice in the classroom

A Reception classroom of children at different stages of development is an environment rich with opportunities for research collaboration. Taking a socio-cultural view of learning collaboration is clearly at the heart of effective learning (Vygotsky, 1978). I believe that some Reception classes are able to move beyond simply supporting collaboration to enabling children to become members of a community of practice. Theorising about learning during the late 1980s and early 1990s by Lave and Wenger emphasised learning by taking part in daily life. They created a model of situated learning that focuses on engagement in a 'community of practice'. Wenger et al. (2002, p.4) defines 'Communities of practice are groups of people who share a concern or a passion for something they do and learn how to do it better as they interact regularly'. This is sometimes taken to suggest that a community of practice is a useful label for a group of like-minded people. As Gherardi et al. (1998, p.279) argue:

> *Referring to a community of practice is not a way to postulate the existence of a new informal grouping or social system within the organisation, but is a way to emphasize that every practice is dependent on social processes through which it is sustained and perpetuated, and that learning takes place through the engagement in that practice.*

This is more helpful in thinking about your Reception class research community. Your community of practice is yourself and the children who together do things that you care about and become better at through this sharing. The best collaboration between young children and their teachers fits this model very well. Here again we can use the Miró Project to exemplify this concept of a 'Community of Practice'. Starting at a similar point of knowledge and understanding, the children and their teachers researched together to find out more about Miró and to then develop their skills as artists. As the project grew, so did their interactions, and an all-consuming passion to find out more. Their community of practice widened as they shared their findings with friends and families.

Point to ponder

In Chapter 3 the value of social media was highlighted and in the twenty-first century we have the opportunity to become members of communities of practice with others we never actually meet. Consider following a blog, joining a google community or creating and sharing a Pinterest board to bring you into other communities of practice.

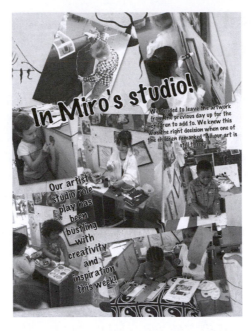

Figure 9.5 Art, from Project Miró, becomes a source of sharing ideas

Persistence in learning and research

The life skill of persistence is one that Reception teachers are ideally placed to support, using continuous provision, exceptional resources and the outdoor learning environment for example. The quality of persistence for effective learning is strongly supported by many authors, not least Claxton who has written about it in many contexts (1997, 1999, 2002, 2013). Many of the readers of this book will have worked or will in future work with children who turn away from things they feel they cannot achieve or who walk away from first unsuccessful efforts. This can be one of the saddest things in the working day and one we work hard to avoid. Each teacher has a range of strategies of their own to build confidence in young learners but understanding the roots of the lack of persistence is also useful. It is sometimes suggested that a culture of instant gratification leads children to have high expectations and low tolerance of failure (Palmer, 2007). This may be true but as well as children turning away from challenge, Reception teachers also see children absorbed and engaged in their learning. This reminds us that children can persist, they are able to concentrate and keep going at things that interest them. The UK guidance for provision for children from birth to five, the Early Years Foundation Stage or EYFS (DfE, 2012), sets out what it calls the 'characteristics of effective learning' to be 'play and exploration', 'active learning' and 'creativity and critical thinking'. In other chapters these characteristics have been considered but the context of supporting persistence in young learner researchers is also important. Each characteristic of effective learning includes something which relates to persistence, though that word is not used. So what are the things you can help children learn which will build their persistence? They need to learn to have a go at a wide range of tasks, some of which are unfamiliar. They also need to be encouraged to know that learning is not always easy and explore the virtue of trying. Ensuring that we praise effort as well as attainment, that ideas are considered and tested out and frustration is a normal experience can all help young learners to be more positive and engaged when the going gets tough. The skilful interactions of the teacher, discussed in relation to sustained shared thinking, model persistent research behaviour to young learners.

The emotional climate of the classroom

Having considered some of the skills young children bring to their research in the classroom, this section goes further into the atmosphere for research and learning that we create as teachers. The emotional climate in the classroom can serve to foster children's research and the development of a community of practice or it can stifle it, making risk, experimentation or persistence unlikely. This climate for learning is sometimes called the classroom culture and that expression does help to make clear the depth and individuality of different classrooms. Good Reception teachers remember that often actions speak louder than words and so modelling to children the desired behaviours is key. That will not be enough to create the climate we want in our classrooms. The climate in which children will thrive is one where children are valued as individuals but also feel part of a group; where being yourself is valued but behaviours are expected that respect the needs of all; where a wide range of emotional states are understood but these are not allowed to impact on the wellbeing of others and where independent thinking is valued. Every Reception teacher considers what the emotional climate of their classroom should be. One of the tools which bears on this issue is Maslow's (1968) hierarchy of needs, though other ways of looking at meeting children's needs have been developed since then. Maslow reminds us that more basic needs have to be met before children are able to move towards the self actualisation which is characterised by flow.

Csikszentmihalyi (1991) writes of the state of flow as an intensely focused, perhaps blissful, and very engaged state of mind. I believe that this state is recognisable in young learners and that the best Reception teachers promote and acknowledge it in their practice by allowing children to work on topics without time restriction so they can be so immersed in accomplishing some task that they lose awareness of all other things, including time. It takes a brave teacher to do this in the face of timetables, curricula and anxious management! Allowing this extension to learning might not be something for every day but should be something for every child. Our children need time when they learn because their minds have been free to wander and settle on something that absorbs them.

In addition to being able to identify and be dedicated to what they want to learn and research about, children also need to be in a state of well-being to be able to do this. Ways to understand well-being are offered by many authors. Laevers (2006, p.15) says 'feeling at home', 'being oneself' and/or 'feeling happy', feeling like 'fish in water'. This seems to have resonance to the notion of flow mentioned above. Others suggest well-being is the realisation of potential in the individual. It has also been described as '…a child's capacity to grow and to develop her/his gifts, to manage life's challenges, to care and be cared for, to influence his/her surroundings in ways that enhance life for all and to delight in one's enjoyment of life' (Gordon 2008 in Moreno, 2008, p.7). What does this mean in our researching Reception class? Children are unlikely to take risks in their learning unless they do feel like a 'fish in water'; new ideas arise when challenge is high and anxiety or stress is low. This sounds like the classroom of an aspirational Reception teacher.

The teacher as researcher

Reflection is the teacher's best friend in both training to teach and developing as a teacher (Ghaye, 2011; Pollard, 2008; Claxton, 1999). Using reflective skills to undertake action research in the classroom is a natural development for many and an effective strategy to consider if you are seeking to make changes or address challenges in your classroom. The informal research that we call reflection can be moved to a more structured approach, which is derived through action research methodology. A useful crystallisation of many more lengthy explanations of action research was provided by Kemmis and McTaggart (1981, p.2) and still stands the test of time. They see action research as a spiral of action, monitoring, evaluation and replanning. This highlights the use of action research in the classroom to address issues and make changes, perhaps in a more systematic way than reflection alone might sustain. The lengthier model of Cohen, Manion and Morrison (2000, pp.235–7) can also be useful and meets the needs of those who want a closely structured stepwise approach to research in their classrooms. McNiff (2010, p.5) provides a lovely clear explanation, saying 'Action research is a practical way of looking at your work in any profession to check that it is as you would like it to be'. So why should you be an action researcher? Unlike traditional research that systematically focuses on finding out about things and how they work, action research is about taking action to improve things. Action research works well for people who are part of the system they are researching, as you are in your Reception class.

McNiff (2010, p.11) makes clear the value of action research in developing and sustaining professionalism. As a teacher you are accountable to lots of people: the parents of children you teach, your phase leader, the head teacher of your school and the education authority your setting is based in. Action research acknowledges the fact that you are accountable to yourself too as a dedicated professional. In its simplest terms action research is a process of steps that make explicit the process of reflection and makes visible the impact of reflection. It always starts with you identifying an issue in your current practice and writing it down along with why it matters to you and your class. Now you need to turn this into a question – it might be a 'how can I' question or a 'what would happen if I' question. It is up to you to frame a question that makes sense to you and it is always good to have a peer or mentor to run it past. Their feedback will help you to be sure that your focus is clear and the topic relevant and not too much to take on at once! Next you will spend a period monitoring what is happening and collecting data about it (one of the key differences between your reflections and your action research). It is good to set a time limit for this phase or you can easily be distracted and the research can drag on. If it takes too long the outcome might be out of date by the time you clarify it. You need to think about how to make secure judgements about your data and how it becomes evidence of improvement or otherwise. Here your reflective skills will help you but you will be recording them again systematically. Once you have evaluated the evidence then you can begin to change practice and reshape your thinking to take things forward. That's all there is to it! An example of effective classroom-based action research follows.

Vignette

In the early days my children would come into the classroom and then get a book to share with a friend until registration and the 'real work' began. Yet in the morning parents would often need a quick word about something which was worrying them. However, I would get increasingly anxious and agitated as the children would be getting restless. Reflecting with my nursery nurse we recognised that this was not an effective use of the children's time. The question which arose was, 'how can children become engaged in learning straightaway'? Having read an article on self-registration we quickly put this into practice and then had a whole range of experiences available for the children to access, for example to support children in developing their dexterity. We planned for one of us to make observations of the children's learning (our way of collecting data) and the other to be available to welcome the children and to be available to talk to parents. Parents were encouraged in to the classroom to settle their children. The impact was clear. Before the change the observations of the children would have been negative. With the changes the observations were detailed and informative. Children were happy and engaged, parents commented positively and we began our day in a more relaxed manner. Aware of the huge impact of these changes we shared our findings with the rest of the school.

The classroom through the lens

The increase in tablet devices in the classroom has made the use of recorded practice for reflection and research much more common. As mentioned earlier this has been undertaken systematically by others, but it is also accessible to the individual Reception teacher. It is fast, cheap and usually in your own control. It is also increasingly something understood by Reception children, who may have been videoed at sports events, at birthday parties and at family events for example. This can generate the problem of the cheesy grin but once your class are used to you using video they are likely to virtually ignore it. There are some questions to be asked about the use of video though and the important ones are:

- When and how can you use video collection to produce data for basic research on teaching and learning processes in your classroom?

- How can you and your class learn with and from video of your community of practice?

- What do you need to think about in deciding when to video and if/how to keep it? (This includes ethical considerations.)

- How can you plan for – and what are the constraints and limitations on – sharing video from your classroom?

Tablet use by children in Reception classes seems to be increasing as does digital assessment. Capturing what happens in your classroom is less edgy than it used to be. Small snapshots of your teaching are a very valuable tool for reflection and putting the camera or table in the hands of one of the children will give a fresh perspective on how you speak, move, model behaviours and more. Peer or mentor feedback is not always necessary – sometimes seeing myself waving my hands around has been enough to remind me to focus my movements more closely to match my words! Allowing children to make a recording or a series of images of their favourite areas of the room is a great revelation. There is much more about this in Chapter 5. I would argue that ethics is a greater concern in visual capture and research when the main participants are children. You will need to think about negotiating 'informed consent' with children if your recording is 'research'. If this is the case then you will be the adult gate-keeper of what is recorded, if and how it is shared. On the other hand you might be using the recording to share with the class or for professional reflection and so only temporary or informal consent will be needed. I believe this rests with your professional judgement. The use of video technology to capture classroom practice is a powerful self-evaluation tool for you and for the children. It can help to show a detailed view of learning and teaching as it happens. In terms of your continuous professional development, using video to view and review learning and teaching promotes self-reflection and can ultimately lead to changes in practice.

Use of research and CPD

Undertaking professional development should provide empowerment for teachers. Being a reflective practitioner is emphasised in teacher preparation and practice, we advocate it as a way of identifying areas for improvement on a wider scale through continuing professional development. At some times in your career this will be through formal training, a particular session on a relevant topic or a course to contribute to your curriculum vitae. It might be less formal, such as observing another teacher in a specific subject area or through peer observation and feedback. The very best CPD comes from your own desire to know more, and you are most likely to identify it for yourself. Sometimes something that is intellectually challenging is just what you need, at other times your confidence might be boosted by revisiting something more familiar. Whichever kind of CPD opportunity is offered to you or you find for yourself, there are some things that can be done to make best use of it. The time has already been committed to identify something, but time also needs to be committed to resourcing it, reflecting on it, sharing with others and hearing their views. Without these extra opportunities the learning may disappear into a black hole with half of your uni-fix cubes and all the hair scrunchies lost in your classroom. Of course, the response of your peers may not be as positive as your own view, this is all part of professional dialogue and differences do not need to be divisive.

Educational research takes place all the time and some of our best understandings have come from research. Often this is longitudinal or large-scale research, perhaps through funded projects or educational charities. As an aspirational Reception teacher you need to have an ear to the ground for what is happening in educational research.

Team talks and tasks

In your class team or phase team find out who is a member of an Early Years professional association, who subscribes to relevant twitter feeds or has newsletters from interesting organisations. Try to widen the range of sources of information and plan a way to share interesting things. You might use a blog or other electronic means or simply a notice board.

When new research comes out it is likely someone in your team will hear about it. It will still need to be checked out though, as not all research is good research. It is valuable to have some tools to analyse research and how you do that will depend on the research you are looking at. Most evaluation of educational research concerns itself with methodology and sample but it is very important to evaluate research in terms of its ethics. One very particular way of looking at research is undertaken by the Educational Endowment Foundation. The Education Endowment Foundation (EEF) is an independent charity dedicated to breaking the link between family income and educational achievement. Their overall intent is to find ways to ensure all children from all backgrounds can fulfil their potential and make the most of their talents. This means that they have an interest in effective pedagogy and as a result of this they both fund and evaluate research. With the Sutton Trust they have created a tool that summarises UK and international research to provide guidance for teachers and schools on how best to use their resources to improve the attainment of pupils. It is certainly something used by head teachers and it may be of interest to teachers too.

Point to ponder

Access the Education Endowment Foundation toolkit at https://educationen dowmentfoundation.org.uk/toolkit/toolkit-a-z/ and see which of the tools is relevant to the Reception class. Do you think that the ideas presented there contribute anything to your understanding of what works best for four year olds?

Sometimes as a teacher is it hard to be an active and effective consumer of educational research. You need to have some ideas about how to understand research that you find out about and use this to support your development as a teacher. Historically, when people wanted to know the best way to do something they consulted (or perhaps observed) someone who could already do it! This was indeed the basis of the monitorial system of teaching in the early days of mass education. In the digital age advice and example comes from a much wider range of sources. Peer-reviewed research journals provide a window on what practitioners are doing to research their own practice as well as academics. You still need to be able to judge good, robust research from that which is less reliable. In 2001 Gersten (2001) noted, both seasoned and novice teachers were 'deluged with misinformation' (p.45). Digital sources have made this even more so. Reception teachers, like other teachers, need ways to evaluate the credibility of these many and varied sources of information. Here are a few suggestions to help you to do this.

- Select refereed journals particularly relevant to Reception practice as many journals and the articles in them will be for a wider audience.

- Look particularly at 'special issues' of journals which bring together research on a topic and see a critical mass of articles on a topic.

- Look at subsequent issues to see if feedback or comment on research articles has been published; you will see if articles are challenged or applauded.

- Focus on empirical work, done through observations of different kinds and allow yourself not to believe things that seem unbelievable! Intellectual honesty is not universal!

- Look at case studies and qualitative data, the best research does not have to be done on a large scale.

- Question what you read. What does it mean for me and my class are questions well worth asking.

Conclusion

You and your Reception class are a unique research community. Enjoy the journeys that they can take you on. For the most part, be a ruthless pragmatist. Be confident that in your own environment some explanations of what you observe are better than others and some ways of doing things are better than others. There is a real world out beyond the classroom and it is a world in flux that will impact on you and the children in your class, it will impact on educational policy and practice. However, there are valid, if fallible and personal, ways of finding out which educational practices are best in your classroom. I believe that researchers and educators are kindred spirits in their approach to knowledge, and that there can be genuine benefits when research knowledge brings light to the classroom.

Further inspiration

Recorded observations have continued to be a valuable tool for teachers and a more recent study well worth learning more about is the 'CIndLe project' – the Cambridgeshire Independent Learning project is reported in an article by Whitebread, Anderson, Coltman, Page, Pasternak and Metha in the journal *Education 3–13* (2005) Volume 33, pages 40–50. More information about the project is also found at http://www.educ.cam.ac.uk/cindle/index.html (last accessed January 2016). The project looked in depth at children's self-regulation strategies as developing learners and at metacognition. Lots of interesting information can be found via the weblink.

Nurture your Reception teacher soul by looking at a book called *First-hand experience: what matters to children* (2014) by Diane Rich, Mary Jane Drummond, Cathy Myer with Annabelle Dixon. They call it an alphabet of learning from the real world, and it will excite and inspire you.

Look out for new information from a research project: 'Classroom talk, social disadvantage and educational attainment: raising standards, closing the gap'. It is a two-year project that started in 2014 and will finish in 2016, which is supported by the Educational Endowment Foundation and directed by Alexander and Hardman. It is a collaboration between the Cambridge Primary Review Trust and the Institute for Effective Education at the University of York. It proposes to develop a range of intervention strategies for training, teaching and mentoring based on Robin Alexander's dialogic teaching work. It is focused on improving learner engagement and raising standards of attainment. Further information can be found at: http://educationendowmentfoundation.org.uk/projects/improving-talk-for-teaching-and-learning/ (last accessed January 2016).

'Attitude is Everything', this is a phrase which I came across a number of years ago in an interesting article about mathematics learning by Zoe Rhydderch-Evans: Attitude is everything (*Mathematics Teaching*, Volume 181, December 2002).

References

Alexander, R. (2004) *Towards dialogic teaching: rethinking classroom talk*. York: Dialogos.

Claxton, G. (1997) *Hare Brain Tortoise Mind*. London: Fourth Estate.

Claxton, G. (1999) *Wise Up: Learning to live the learning life*. Stafford: Network Educational Press.

Claxton, G. (2002) *Building learning power: Helping young people become better learners*. Bristol: TLO.

Claxton, G. (2007) Expanding young people's capacity to learn. *British Journal of Educational Studies*, 55 (2): 115–34.

Claxton, G. (2013) http://www.winchester.ac.uk/aboutus/lifelonglearning/CentreforReal WorldLearning/Documents/Claxton%20%282013%29%20School%20as%20an%20 epistemic%20apprenticeship%20%28Vernon%20Wall%29.pdf [last accessed January 2016]

Cohen, L., Manion, L. and Morrison K. (2000) *Research methods in education*. Abingdon: Routledge.

Csikszentmihalyi, M. (1991) *Flow: The psychology of optimal experience*. New York: Harper Perennial.

De Bono, E. (1985) *De Bono's thinking course.* London: Ariel Books.

De Bono, E. (1988) *Letters to thinkers: Further thoughts on lateral thinking.* London: Penguin Books.

Department for Education (DfE) (2012) *Statutory Framework for the Early Years Foundation Stage.* Runcorn: Department for Education.

Eick, C.J. and Reed, C.J. (2002) What makes an inquiry oriented science teacher? The influence of learning histories on student teacher role identity and practice. *Science Teacher Education*, 86: 401–16.

Galton, M., Hargreaves, L., Comber, C., Pell, T. and Wall, D. (1999) *Inside the primary classroom: 20 years on.* London: Routledge.

Gersten, R. (2001) Sorting out the roles of research in the improvement of practice. *Learning Disabilities: Research & Practice*, 16 (1): 45–50.

Ghaye, T. (2011) *Teaching and learning through reflective practice: A practitioner guide for positive action (2nd ed.).* London: Routledge.

Gherardi, S., Nicolini, D. and Odella, F. (1998) Toward a social understanding of how people learn in organizations. *Management Learning*, 29 (3): 273–97.

Gordon J. (2008) 'A sense of belonging as part of children's well-being' in *Early Childhood Matters*, 111: 7–12.

Kemmis, S. and McTaggart, R. (1981) *The action research planner.* Victoria: Deakin University.

Laevers, F. (2006) *A process-oriented child monitoring system for young children.* Leuven, Belgium: CEGO Publishers.

McNiff, J. (2010) *Action research for professional development.* Dorset: September Books.

Maslow, A. (1968) *Towards a psychology of being (2nd ed.).* New York: Van Nostrand.

Murray, J. (2013) Young children's research behaviour? Children aged four to eight years finding solutions at home and at school. *Early Child Development and Care,* 183 (8): 1147–65.

Palmer, S. (2007) *Toxic childhood: How the modern world is damaging our children and what we can do about it.* London: Orion.

Perkins, D. (1995) *Outsmarting IQ: the emerging science of learnable intelligence.* New York: Free Press.

Pollard, A. (2008) *Reflective teaching: Evidence informed professional practice* (3rd ed.). London: Continuum.

Siraj-Blatchford, I., Sylva, K., Muttock, S., Gilden, R. and Bell, D. (2002) *Researching Effective Pedagogy in the Early Years* (REPEY) DfES Research Report 365. HMSO London: Queen's Printer.

Vygotsky, L. (1978) *Mind and society: The development of higher mental process.* Cambridge, MA: Harvard University Press.

Wenger. E., McDermott, R. and Snyder, W. (2002) *Cultivating communities of practice.* Boston, MA: Harvard Business School Press.

Jottings

10 The mirror in the hat shop

Anna Cox and Gillian Sykes

In this short chapter we bring together ideas from the previous chapters and discuss the idea of a personal pedagogy. Some ideas for the future are proposed and we go back to the hat shop.

Introduction

We anticipate that you will not have read this book from front to back but will have dipped in to the things that excite you first, come to other parts of the book in response to things happening in your studies or your classroom and perhaps then filled in the gaps. It is a bit like that when you are building your personal professional pedagogy. Some things come from what lit the fire of aspiration to be a Reception teacher, some things about the teacher you want to be, (perhaps need to be), come from formative experiences and then you will have picked up and developed things along the way. That is the way it has been for members of the writing team for this book too. And we keep on learning and developing our pedagogy, it is more like a moving river of ever changing knowledge and experience than a lake to dip into. In the rest of this chapter we talk about aspects of pedagogy and try to set you up for the journey down the river, calling at the hat shop on the way to have a quick look in the mirror.

The curriculum

In whatever context you are teaching four-year-old children there will be a curriculum framework. Individuals feel very differently about the value and purpose of the curriculum.

It should never be a straightjacket, and the confident Reception teacher manages to balance what is right for the children with the curriculum and in your head it will be that way round. Your phase leader, the head teacher, the inspectorate and others might think of it the other way around.

It is interesting to look at the curricula for four year olds in other parts of the world too. For example, you may already know about Te Whāriki, the curriculum for Early Years education in New Zealand, and find its concepts of warp and weft, and the child-centred nature of its approach exciting and yet challenging to understand in your own context.

> **Inspiration point:** Take a look at the http://www.education.govt.nz/early-childhood/teaching-and-learning/ece-curriculum/ last accessed January 2016. Which of the key features of this curriculum are you drawn to? Are any of the features of New Zealand Early Years education embedded in your practice?

Where is your pedagogy today?

Sometimes it can be useful and interesting to audit or review your own pedagogic stance. A lot of the time Reception teachers are busy 'doing' and the underpinnings of their actions are not in the forefront. At the end of a term or a year can be a good time to reflect on the scope of your pedagogy. You could do that through the Jottings pages of this book, in a journal or through a blog.

The roots of your pedagogy probably come from your training but they will have been nurtured by personal beliefs about children and about education, some of which is discussed in our chapter on advocating for Early Years. As times change, political climates change and culture changes, then there will be challenges to what you learnt. That has been the case for the authors of this book. We have found what we were taught, challenged and sometimes overturned. It can be initially unsettling but has been good for us and if it happens to you it will help you to be flexible and grounded as you work out the best way to do your important job.

> **Point to ponder**
>
> Undertake an audit of your pedagogic principles. What is the golden thread that is woven into your practice? What do you believe about children and what you can provide for them? If that seems difficult, try to describe your educational values as a starting point.

Inclusive pedagogy

The notion of inclusive pedagogy has been more implied than explicit in this book. This is partly from our belief that strong professional pedagogies held by those working with four year olds are inclusive. However, it is important at this point to be clear about inclusion. Reception teachers should, and in our experience do, value cultural diversity. At the start of the twenty-first century and at a time of huge population movement this is crucial. This has been developed more fully in Chapter 8.

In working with trainee teachers an expression that we share with them is this – 'If you want to change the world, teach young children'. Your influence and impact will continue long after they leave your class. Many of us as adults remember those first teachers who enabled us to find ourselves. There is nothing wrong with wanting to be that teacher the children remember but it is more important that they remember that there was a climate of social justice in your classroom, that respect and care were practised by you and encouraged in them. Your understanding of child development and your personal values will shape this but so will your understanding of the wider community around the setting and the communities within it. That is one of the reasons that inclusive pedagogy, pedagogy in general, must be open to change. You will be the teacher that your class needs and that is not the same every year.

Figure 10.1 Nurture is part of the Reception teacher's role

Nurturing your Reception teacher soul

Networks, communities of practice and social media have all been mentioned as supportive to you as Reception teacher. In this section we think more about how you can continue to motivate yourself, how to find inspiration and how to balance being a Reception teacher with other areas of your life. Most of those working with young children are attracted by beautiful things, things that the children we teach will be stimulated and engaged by. Some of us on the writing team still need to have those things while others are not so squirrel like and find ways to access things without owning them! You will need to decide if you are going to allow yourself to hoard or if you are not. Making this decision early is important. It is lovely to have the basket of shells, the fossil and the dinosaur egg, but perhaps they don't need to live at home. Schools vary in the resources they may be able to offer you or store, so that must be taken into account too. Increasingly we are able to take children to art galleries, museums, to the woods or to a performance and bring them and ourselves into contact with wondrous things – so hoarding is not essential. Again this is discussed in more detail in Chapter 8.

There is a saying that 'the road up and the road down are the same road' and that may be true for car drivers. In teaching the road up is not the same as the road down; the things that motivate and energise Reception teachers are not the same as those that can lead to less positive feelings. This is the same for most professional groups (Hertzberg, 1987). The things that are on the road up and which motivate need to be cultivated and enjoyed. When you give so much of yourself to your class as Reception teachers do, it is important to 'top up'. It is up to you to find the things in your work that provide the positives and there are many of them. There is a different challenge to deal with the 'road down' as the contributors to this often prove to be external. It might be the arrival of an inspection team, a staff meeting that runs too long so that you miss your gym session or something you hear on the radio about education. These things need to be handled too. They probably can't be changed but they can be put in perspective with the help of all those 'road up' things. No one working with Reception children in a busy school can expect it all to be plain sailing but the lows and highs are there to make the journey interesting.

Let's not forget about well-being

We talk in loud voices about supporting children's well-being. How well-being supports involvement and engagement. How children need to be in the flow, and feel like 'a fish in water'. We are confident in knowing that this is true. Yet who tells us that Reception teachers need to be 'mind minded'? Who helps us to feel like a 'fish in water'? Faced with changes in policy and legislation, a battering by the media, along with the demands the head and regulatory bodies place on us often leaves us feeling 'undervalued'. Hence we need to look after our own well-being. Think about Maslow's Hierarchy of Needs. Are we ensuring that we have our physiological needs met? Are we eating healthily and drinking regularly (not the alcoholic kinds)? Are we having enough sleep and having regular exercise? Do we feel safe and secure in our workplace and home life? If not, what can we do about it? Do we feel a sense of belonging? Do people listen to us and value our ideas and views? If these needs are being met we should then be able to self-actualise in both work and play.

Being a Reception teacher you work hard at being the best you can for the children, their families, your team, other agencies and of course the people that you care about outside school. Often this is what keeps us going (the fuel in our engines). However, sometimes we need more than this. The fuel in our engines needs to be topped up. Be kind to yourselves. Go for a walk, eat something delicious, bake a cake, learn something new, go to the gym, meet a friend for a natter, read a book, dance, sing. Wear a hat that you don't wear in school!

The mirror in the hat shop

Earlier in this book we imagined the Reception teacher putting on and taking off hats; now at the end is a good time to revisit the hat shop and look in the mirror. This might be a good time for some cognitive reframing. By that we mean reflecting on your role and entertaining different ways of being, strategies and thoughts about what you do. You can't do this in that state of emotional flood that Eleonora talked about in Chapter 2.

As a Reception teacher sometimes you need to use your posture, your location in the room and your facial expressions to change an emotional state. Sometimes you do this for an external audience, an angry parent for example, but it can end up reducing your own emotional state in quite an unhelpful way too. At other times, you will be able to maintain positive intentions as a means of staying centred and managing your emotions.

Thinking about yourself as an adult and as a teacher is a challenging thing to do. Kegan (1982, 1994) postulated three stages of adult development, which he calls socialising, self-authoring and self-transformational. The socialising stage is represented by traditional thinking, for a teacher this is likely to be as a result of training and early professional experience. It is a stage which involves being surrounded by and responding to norm, ideas and thinking prevalent among other people. Kegan's second phase is self-authoring and he suggests that only about 50 per cent of people achieve this. It is when contemporary ideas are challenged by the individual and personal deeply held values are developed. Internal rules guide the behaviour of self-authoring individuals and they are more self-guided and self-evaluative as well as self-motivated. This sounds much like the aspirational Reception teacher, in our view. Now is a good time to aspire to the third of Kegan's stages of adult development and become self-transformational. He suggests that not many people manage this and that most of them are over 40! How good it would be to see Reception teachers buck that trend. You can be open to contradictory understandings of the world; you can appreciate ambiguity and challenge; you can see shades of grey; and you are able to revise and reconstruct your understanding of your professional role and your professional identity. We hope this book will help you do it.

References

Hertzberg, F.I. (1987) One more time: how do you motivate employees? *Harvard Business Review*, September/October, 65(5): 109–20.

Kegan, R. (1982) *The evolving self: Problems and processes in human development*. Cambridge, MA: Harvard University Press.

Kegan, R. (1994) *In over our heads: the mental demands of modern life*. Cambridge, MA: Harvard University Press.

Index